CAN YOU HANDLE
THE TRUTH?

R.T. KENDALL
ANDREW SAMPSON

CAN YOU
HANDLE
THE TRUTH?

PERSPECTIVES ON 2 TIMOTHY

CWR

Concept development, editing, design and production by CWR
Printed in Finland by WS Bookwell
ISBN-13: 978-1-85345-377-9
ISBN-10: 1-85345-377-3

CONTENTS

FOREWORD

Rev Dr Rob Frost (Director of Share Jesus International and Leader of 'Easter People')

This book is the result of a remarkable collaboration. It is written by two outstanding biblical expositors, one of whom has been a leader in this field for over 40 years and the other who is 'just starting out'. One represents 'the post-war generation' and the other 'Generation X'. One is categorised as 'young', the other (quite mistakenly!) 'old'.

These studies came as the result of a powerful partnership at Easter People. I asked them to lead the main morning Bible studies as a team together. It was, initially, a difficult and challenging task for them – but one which they ultimately found deeply enriching. It was a partnership which the thousands of people who heard them speak each morning described as 'rich', 'outstanding' and 'brilliant'!

These Bible studies modelled something extremely important in the life of the Church. They demonstrated that in a society in which the generations are separated by culture, language and self-interest – the kingdom of God is broad enough to hold us together. When people at different stages of life minister together in fellowship, partnership and love, they show the breadth of God's kingdom.

The mission of the Church is something which crosses the generations. When we pray, work and minister together at different stages of life God can use us powerfully. In working together we say something significant about 'belonging' to a broken and divided world which we can't say when we're apart.

Cross-generational ministry is significant because those who take the risk of doing it bring different perspectives, language styles and cultural experiences to the same table. They speak to a wider audience together than they can ever address apart.

Andrew and RT are modelling the way in which the different generations need each other. Those just starting out need the wisdom and mentorship of older Christians so as to avoid the pitfalls of the journey ahead. Those who are older need the enthusiasm, vision and energy of the rising generation so as to keep focused and to 'finish well'.

This kind of cross-generational ministry is nothing new; Paul and Timothy showed the importance of it, and the perspectives shared here demonstrate the kind of mentoring and encouraging ministry which Paul shared with his young colleague Timothy.

For a long time the generations have been distant from and even at war with each other. Misunderstanding and mistrust have spoilt our relationships. Among the rising generation I find a real desire to reach out to those who've gone before, and a genuine hope that we can find new ways of working together. We have much to learn from each other, and much to do together that we can't do alone. I pray that a new unity across the generations will become a hallmark of the emerging Church.

The content of 2 Timothy fascinates me. It's a letter of encouragement to a young man struggling with a church which is in deep trouble. It's written by an older Christian leader who, himself, is facing persecution and hardship.

I recently led a pilgrimage to Ephesus. It was an inspiring and beautiful time, and one in which the life of the church there really came alive for me. At the end of the pilgrimage the Turkish tour guide accompanied us to the airport. She seemed sad that she was soon to bid us all farewell. As the coach rumbled along the motorway she whispered to me: 'I have one more surprise left. Miletus!'

This comment sent me scrambling for my Bible concordance. Miletus wasn't one of the seven churches of Asia! In fact, I'd never heard of it. But as I turned to Acts 20 I saw how poignant and important a place it was. It was where Paul said his last goodbye to the church leaders from Ephesus.

The coach pulled in beside the remains of a huge Roman fortress. The sea had long receded, and this once great port was now nothing more than a crumbling ruin. Paul arrived by sea to meet the Ephesian leaders at this once bustling port. He had already caused a riot in Ephesus and he didn't want to cause further problems for them ... so that's why he arranged this secret farewell meeting at Miletus.

The leaders from Ephesus were under great threat, and Paul also looked to his own future with an impending sense that suffering was imminent. The 30 pilgrims on my tour followed me past the ruined fort to the place where boats like Paul's would once have been moored. We ambled across the rough scrubland to an old weather-beaten tree where we stopped to say our good-byes, to pray for one another and to end our pilgrim trail.

There, in the shadow of a sprawling tree, as the midday sun scorched the ground all around, I read Paul's words:

And now, compelled by the Spirit, I am going to Jerusalem, not knowing what will happen to me there. I only know that in every city the Holy Spirit warns me that prison and hardships are facing me. However, I consider my life worth nothing to me, if only I may finish the race and complete the task the Lord Jesus has given me – the task of testifying to the gospel of God's grace. Now I know that none of you among whom I have gone about preaching the kingdom will ever see me again. (Acts 20:22–25)

My group of pilgrims ... black and white, old and young, poor and prosperous ... sheltered in the shade of a large tree. They shared the challenges which faced each one of them back home and prayed for one another. I was moved to tears. Some of them faced personal suffering back home; a suffering implicit in caring for someone who made enormous demands, a suffering caused by choosing a life of integrity resulting in alienation at work, a suffering wrought by persisting with a difficult relationship when others would have discarded it, a suffering caused by forgiving even more than seventy times seven.

In that moment the experiences of our time in Ephesus together were crystallised. In the footsteps of Paul we had discovered that suffering really is part of the discipleship deal for all of us, whatever our life back home. I left the shade of the gnarled old tree with a new commitment to follow Christ whatever the cost.

Paul's instruction to Timothy expounded in this book gives us important clues as to how we should live in a Church so often compromised, divided, secularised and weak. This letter to Timothy, written 'across the generations', speaks powerfully to the needs of our age. Paul has not written from the cloistered silence of a college library, his teaching has been hammered into shape by the anvil of suffering, persecution and heartbreak. It has much to say to us, today.

CHAPTER ONE

2 TIMOTHY 1

ANOINTING – THROUGH SUFFERING
R.T. KENDALL

FINDING YOUR PLACE IN THE
PURPOSES OF GOD
ANDREW SAMPSON

2 TIMOTHY 1

¹ Paul, an apostle of Christ Jesus by the will of God, according to the promise of life that is in Christ Jesus,

² To Timothy, my dear son:
Grace, mercy and peace from God the Father and Christ Jesus our Lord.

Encouragement to Be Faithful
³ I thank God, whom I serve, as my forefathers did, with a clear conscience, as night and day I constantly remember you in my prayers.

⁴ Recalling your tears, I long to see you, so that I may be filled with joy.

⁵ I have been reminded of your sincere faith, which first lived in your grandmother Lois and in your mother Eunice and, I am persuaded, now lives in you also.

⁶ For this reason I remind you to fan into flame the gift of God, which is in you through the laying on of my hands.

⁷ For God did not give us a spirit of timidity, but a spirit of power, of love and of self-discipline.

⁸ So do not be ashamed to testify about our Lord, or ashamed of me his prisoner. But join with me in suffering for the gospel, by the power of God,

⁹ who has saved us and called us to a holy life – not because of

anything we have done but because of his own purpose and grace. This grace was given us in Christ Jesus before the beginning of time,

[10] but it has now been revealed through the appearing of our Saviour, Christ Jesus, who has destroyed death and has brought life and immortality to light through the gospel.

[11] And of this gospel I was appointed a herald and an apostle and a teacher.

[12] That is why I am suffering as I am. Yet I am not ashamed, because I know whom I have believed, and am convinced that he is able to guard what I have entrusted to him for that day.

[13] What you heard from me, keep as the pattern of sound teaching, with faith and love in Christ Jesus.

[14] Guard the good deposit that was entrusted to you – guard it with the help of the Holy Spirit who lives in us.

[15] You know that everyone in the province of Asia has deserted me, including Phygelus and Hermogenes.

[16] May the Lord show mercy to the household of Onesiphorus, because he often refreshed me and was not ashamed of my chains.

[17] On the contrary, when he was in Rome, he searched hard for me until he found me.

[18] May the Lord grant that he will find mercy from the Lord on that day! You know very well in how many ways he helped me in Ephesus.

ANOINTING – THROUGH SUFFERING

R.T. KENDALL ON 2 TIMOTHY 1

The second epistle to Timothy is almost certainly Paul's last letter, and its main focus is his teaching on the integrity of the gospel. There were vital reasons why Paul wanted to make sure that everything he said to his protégé, Timothy, was stated clearly. He knew this was it! And since this is Paul's 'last word' we need to take seriously what he has to say. We need to understand what was important to him – not what is important to us. When you read the Bible don't look for what just excites you, but seek to find out why the passage was written.

But while the main theme of 2 Timothy is the integrity of the gospel there is a subsidiary theme: suffering. It comes out in each of the four chapters, as we shall see. Why is suffering so important? Because it is the way to a greater anointing.

'Join me in suffering' (v.8)

I would rather have a greater anointing than anything. I would be willing to push a peanut with my nose across London if I thought it would result in a greater anointing! The anointing is the power of the Holy Spirit which enables us to do what we do with ease. Once we come to a point where the going is hard and we are struggling, we've gone outside our anointing. The anointing is the place of least fatigue. Burnout is often caused by someone going outside their anointing – doing what God didn't call them to do and pretending to be something that they are not. However, if we want an increased anointing then it is almost certain that God will allow us to go through suffering. That's why Paul says in verse 8 of this chapter, '… join with me in suffering for the gospel'.

The good news is that the greater the suffering the greater the anointing. And we all need a greater anointing – not just ministers or evangelists. If you are a doctor or a lorry driver you need an anointing to do what you do and to do it well, but to do it with ease.

Are you suffering? If you are, you may feel that you have every reason to feel sorry for yourself, especially if it's a time of great trial you are going through. Everyone has a story to tell about this. Suppose we are in a gathering and people start sharing their experiences of suffering. One tells of being lied about, and that people believed it. Someone else tells of being abused as a child and never having got over it. Another shares how a marriage partner has been unfaithful to them. Someone tells of the pain of losing their job, yet another of how a church leader has let them down. When everyone has told their tales of woe a vote is taken to decide on the top ten of those who have suffered most. Then it is decided to narrow it down to the top three and, finally, to the one who has suffered more than anyone else. Suppose it is you and when you are called on to the platform the leader of the meeting greets you with 'Congratulations!' You say, 'Well, thanks a lot!' What, in fact, you have been handed is an invitation on a silver platter to come up higher and receive such an anointing of God that few people experience. Instead of your suffering being the rationale for self-pity it is the way to glory!

'God did not give us a spirit of timidity' (v.7)

Suffering, and greater anointing, is for the sake of the gospel. In this chapter Paul focuses on the power of the gospel. Through it, Paul says 'God did not give us a spirit of timidity' (fear), 'but a spirit of power, of love, and of self-discipline' (v.7). There are certain needs built in to every human being and they came to us by virtue of creation. We read in Genesis 1:27 that 'God created man in his own image, in the image of God he created him; male and female he created them'. God created us to need affection, affirmation and attention. It is through the gospel that He gives these things to us – meeting needs that people have not satisfied, for people, including our parents and authority figures, can let us down.

Paul knew something about Timothy, his personality and background. Timothy was a very fearful person – you could say he had low self-esteem, an inferiority complex. In telling the Corinthians about Timothy's planned visit, Paul urges them to be gentle with him, to make him feel at home, to be sensitive towards him (1 Cor. 16:10–11). If you are ruled by timidity, by a spirit of fear, the gospel will give you the significance and affirmation that you are looking for.

There's a verse in the Bible that has governed me more than anything else. It's John 5:44, 'How can you believe if you accept praise from one another, yet make no effort to obtain the praise that comes from the only God?' In other words, you're looking for significance, wanting self-esteem and you think that you'll feel better about yourself if people say the right things to you. The truth is that if you seek significance that way you'll never find it – only the gospel can satisfy us.

Paul wants us to know that God has not given us a spirit of fear. Something I learned from Dr Martyn Lloyd-Jones many years ago was that God never oppresses us. Any oppression comes from the flesh and the devil. If you are motivated by fear, understand that it does not come from God. I don't mean reverential fear of God; that's different – and necessary. What I am saying is that God doesn't want you to be afraid and He doesn't want you to doubt His love for you. Jesus said it to the disciples: 'Do not let your hearts be troubled. Trust in God; trust also in me' (John 14:1). If you look at the context, you will see that Jesus said these words after an exchange with Peter, who had declared, 'I will lay down my life for you.' Jesus' response to that was, 'Will you really lay down your life for me? I tell you the truth, before the cock crows, you will disown me three times!' (John 13:37–38). So in telling Peter and the other disciples, 'Do not let your hearts be troubled,' Jesus demonstrates that, even though God knows we will let Him down, He loves us. You are loved with an everlasting love. If you're struggling, trying to perform, grasp this truth and then hear God say, in effect, 'Ah, that's better; now I can really love you!'

It's amazing that although Jesus knew Peter would disown him in just a few hours, He could say, 'It's OK. Don't be troubled.' He knows us through and through, that we are dust. It cannot be stated enough: fear and timidity do not come from God! John says that 'perfect love drives out fear, because fear has to do with punishment' (1 John 4:18). Fear makes you want to defend yourself, or if somebody does something nasty you immediately want to let it be known what has been done to you. But when you allow God's perfect love to drive out fear you will totally forgive and you won't go around telling everybody what the perpetrator did to you. And when you totally forgive you won't let them be afraid of you. Without forgiving you hope that when you meet them they will be afraid, while in reality you're the one who is afraid. But through the gospel the fear is dealt with and we are affirmed with power, love and self-discipline, or, as the

Authorised Version puts it, 'a sound mind'.

Paul writes in 2 Timothy 1:8 about what the Authorised Version renders as the 'afflictions' of the gospel: 'So do not be ashamed to testify about our Lord, or ashamed of me his prisoner. But join with me in suffering for the gospel' ('afflictions of the gospel'). We are not only called to believe in Him but, equally, to suffer for Him (Phil. 1:29). Paul entrusted Timothy with passing this message on to the church in Thessalonica. He sent him to tell them not to be 'unsettled by these trials. You know quite well that we were destined for them' (1 Thess. 3:3). Like it or not, trials are from God. As the old hymn puts it, 'Every joy or trial cometh from above.'

Trials can be little things – like rushing out of the house and discovering you can't find the car keys, or getting into an argument on the way to a worship service. These things are upsetting and annoying, but God allows them to happen so that He can work in us. So accept any trial. 'In this world you will have trouble,' said Jesus (John 16:33).

The severest trial is when the world hates us because of our allegiance to Him. Jesus said, 'If the world hates you, keep in mind that it hated me first' (John 15:18). A great verse to remember is Mark 8:35: 'For whoever wants to save his life will lose it, but whoever loses his life for me and for the gospel will save it.' How do you cope when the trials, big and small, come? The power of the gospel is sufficient to bring you through.

I talked on this subject in the series I did on 2 Timothy at Easter People (on which these studies are based) and afterwards a dear man tearfully told me that he had been going through much suffering, and he could not believe that God was the cause of such experiences. Yet God *does* take responsibility for our suffering. He could stop it and what He does not stop He allows.

He knows we can take it because 1 Corinthians 10:13 says, 'No temptation has seized you except what is common to man. And God is faithful; he will not let you be tempted beyond what you can bear.' The Greek word for 'temptation' is trial. The two words are used interchangeably.

The question is quite often asked, 'Does God actually instigate suffering?' He did with Job: 'Then the LORD said to Satan, "Have you considered my servant Job?"' He started it, but He would only let the devil go so far (Job 1:8ff). When God allows suffering to come He knows how much we can bear. Sometimes it seems so great that we think we cannot take another day of it, but He knows exactly when to stop it. He's always right on time – never too late, never too early. When He steps in the trial will end – and the result of it will be a greater anointing.[1]

The apostle John showed the right attitude to trial when exiled to the island of Patmos: 'I, John, your brother and companion in the suffering and kingdom and patient endurance that are ours in Jesus' (Rev. 1:9). I came across that verse and found something new in it some years ago when I was going through a severe trial. I realised that John was saying, in effect, 'Look, when you are going through real trial you've been elevated to the big league.' We can dignify trials: 'Consider it pure joy, my brothers, whenever you face trials of many kinds' (James 1:2). Again, it's congratulations! You've been promoted and will receive a greater anointing. There is a work for you that no one else can do. If you are in that severe trial and you're feeling sorry for yourself, God says, 'Don't be. I've not finished with you yet. You have been earmarked for a work that you have no idea of if, in the process, you are not ashamed.'

'Do not be ashamed of me' (v. 8)

In verse 8, Paul instructs Timothy not to be ashamed of the gospel, or of Paul himself. Allegiance to Jesus Christ means allegiance to His people. Sometimes the Christians we know may not be the ones we would choose to go on holiday with, but they are God's people and we must affirm our brothers and sisters. Don't be surprised, however, if those who hurt you most are from the company of, dare I say it, the godly. As the ditty goes:

> Living with the saints above,
> Oh, that will be glory!
> Living with the saints below –
> Well, that's another story.

Sometimes showing allegiance to Christ is demonstrated by the way we affirm those who are unashamed of Him. I've long sought to be close to those I felt had a greater anointing. I want to mix with people like that. And sometimes, like it or not, God chooses some strange people to have a greater anointing! There are times when I look at the church scene in the United Kingdom and wonder who God will use next. Then I see someone He has chosen and think, 'Oh, no!' and I want to be as far away from them as possible. Yet I've learned not to be ashamed to be seen with such people.

Once Colin Dye, Senior Pastor of Kensington Temple, London, said to me, 'RT, how would you like to meet Rodney Howard-Browne?' Swallowing my misgivings, I agreed. Rodney is the man who has been called the Father of the Toronto Blessing. When I first heard about it I thought, 'This is not of God.' The truth was that I didn't want it to be of God because I found the phenomena associated with 'the Blessing' to be offensive – laying hands on people so they fall to the floor and start laughing. I thought 'Oh boy, why would God use a man like this?' But it wasn't long after I started talking with him that I realised he had an anointing. I said to him, 'I wonder what you are doing on Saturday? Would you come to Westminster Chapel? I'd like you to stand in the pulpit and I'd love you to pray for my wife, Louise.'

At the time, in 1993, Louise was suffering from severe depression. She had had a cough for three years and no doctor had found a cure for it. Even a stay in hospital failed to bring about any improvement. It actually tempted me to give up my ministry and go back to America, long before I reached retirement age. But that Saturday morning we met up with Rodney and his wife, Adonica, at Westminster Chapel. There was no hype – no working things up. Louise just sat in a chair tired out, having had little sleep the night before. Rodney and Adonica laid hands on her and she was instantly healed.

People have said to me about Rodney, 'How could you mix with a person like that?' My reply is, because he has an anointing and I am not ashamed of my association with him. That's what Paul means when he says to Timothy, 'Do not be … ashamed of me, his prisoner' (v.8). How would you like it if your mentor were in prison? Don't be ashamed of those who want all of God that they can have.

Life ... through the gospel (v.10)

From dealing with allegiance to the gospel Paul goes on to its power – what the gospel does for us. Through it, the apostle says in verse 9, God 'has saved us and called us to a holy life'. John says, 'Yet to all who received him, to those who believed in his name, he gave the right to become children of God' (John 1:12).

Through being saved we are called to live a holy life, unashamed of the Word of God. The purpose of the gospel isn't to socialise us or politicise us; it is not just to make society better. The gospel brings life and light. It is a reminder that we are going to go to heaven and not to hell when we die and in the meantime we are called to a holy life. The origin of our life lies in God's purpose and grace – not in anything we have done.

Your conversion was no accident. You didn't just happen to meet the right person who told you about Jesus, nor did you just happen to go into a church or an evangelistic meeting. Oh no, says Paul, you were known from the beginning of time – 'All who were appointed for eternal life believed' (Acts 13:48). So understand that God has had His eye on you from before the first speck of dust existed in remotest space. From before the beginning of time He has had his hand on you. The assurance of the gospel is that He has abolished death and lets us know that we're going to go to heaven at the end of our lives on earth. So Paul says to Timothy, 'I am not ashamed, because I know whom I have believed, and am convinced that he is able to guard what I have entrusted to him for that day' (v.12).

The early Methodists made an important contribution to theological knowledge by declaring that a person could know they were saved. John Calvin gave us the teaching of the inner testimony of the Spirit, by which we can know that the Bible is the Word of God, and we can have an assurance of salvation, but the early Methodists went beyond that by saying you could *feel* your sins are forgiven and *know* that you've been born of God. And God wants you to know that.

Are you sure that if you died today you would you go to heaven? If you stood before God and He asked you 'Why should I let you into my heaven?' what would you say? If you do not know that you are saved and can say with Paul 'I know whom I have believed', may God give you no rest until you know that you have the life of God in your soul.

FINDING YOUR PLACE IN THE PURPOSES OF GOD

ANDREW SAMPSON ON 2 TIMOTHY 1

We meet Timothy at a crucial, perhaps the most crucial point in his life. The church in Ephesus, once a centre of godly leadership and apostolic orthodoxy (Acts 20:17–38), has been buffeted by the winds of false teaching and has begun to come apart at the seams. Those with 'sincere faith' (v.5) have dwindled to a minority and 'men of depraved minds' who 'oppose the truth' (3:8) are jostling for influence. Timothy now finds himself like a vulnerable young sapling standing alone in a clearing after a hurricane has felled the mighty oaks that once stood at its side. His mentor and 'father in the Lord', Paul, is imprisoned in Rome awaiting certain execution. Many once loyal to the apostle have deserted him and the gospel he once boldly proclaimed throughout the Mediterranean region (v.15; 2:17–18; 4:10,16). Timothy is alone, young (1 Tim. 4:12a; 2 Tim. 2:22a), apprehensive (vv.7–8; cf.1 Cor. 16:10) and weak in body (1 Tim. 5:23) with the awareness that all his training alongside the towering figure of the apostle has been leading him to this point.

One cannot read this letter without gaining a sense of the gravity of Timothy's situation. The central message is clear: Timothy is not to allow himself to be swept along in the movements of his time, however fashionable they may be and however popular it will make him. This letter is at its heart a call to loyalty – loyalty to the gospel as revealed in Christ (v.10) and proclaimed by Paul (v.11). F.W. Boreham writes movingly about the kind of challenge that now faces Timothy:

> There come times – serious times; critical times; pivotal times; times upon which destiny seems tremblingly to hang – when a man must re-adjust his relationship to the general scheme of things. He must assume control. Instead of being negative, he must be positive; instead of being languidly passive, he must be splendidly active; instead of acquiescing in the movements of his time, he must take charge of them.[2]

Behind Paul's words to his young apprentice is the conviction that the God who appointed Paul as 'a herald and an apostle and a teacher' (v.11, cf.v.1) is now calling Timothy to take control of the situation in Ephesus. This is his God-ordained purpose.

The idea of 'purpose' is central to a biblical worldview. A few months ago I set out to stimulate discussion in my high-ability, mixed-sex class of fourteen-year-olds by asking them the question, 'What is the purpose of life?' Their responses were thoughtful and extremely varied. A couple of students, possibly influenced by the fact they were being quizzed in a science lesson, opted for a biological answer to my question: 'To mate and have babies.' Others suggested a hedonistic answer – 'To have fun' – and an environmental answer: 'To look after the world.' But most common by far was the cheerless response, 'There is no purpose to life.' A large proportion of teenagers do not know what they are living for. They would identify with the words of the Nobel Prize-winning biologist, Jacques Monod, whose work I first read at university and whose thought perfectly characterised the intellectual climate of my department at that time:

... man at last knows that he is alone in the unfeeling immensity of the universe, out of which he emerged only by chance. Neither his destiny nor his duty have been written down.[3]

This view could not be further removed from that of Scripture. The biblical writers are unequivocal about the fact that God has not only ordained a purpose for humankind as a whole (see, eg, Isa. 43:7; Col. 1:16; Heb. 2:10),[4] but that He also creates individual men and women for purposes that are specific and unique. The prophet Isaiah writes, 'Before I was born the LORD called me; from my birth he has made mention of my name' (Isa. 49:1). At his commissioning Jeremiah learns from God, 'Before you were born I set you apart; I appointed you as a prophet to the nations' (Jer. 1:5), and in one of his most beautiful and best-loved psalms David celebrates the fact that 'you knit me together in my mother's womb ... All the days ordained for me were written in your book before one of them came to be' (Psa. 139:13,16). The apostle Paul, too, was convinced that he had been set apart from birth in order to preach Christ to the Gentiles (Gal. 1:15–16), and this in spite of him having spent his early years 'kicking against the goads' (Acts 26:14).[5] It comes as no surprise, then, that Paul is convinced that Timothy has a sacred call on his life to serve in Ephesus as a minister of the gospel, his conviction supported by the prophecies given at Timothy's ordination (1 Tim. 1:18; 4:14). Although it is never stated in so many words, it is not unreasonable to suppose that, in Paul's mind at least, Timothy's 'Yes' to his call amounts to the fulfilment of the purpose for which he was created.

I am aware that for many Christians the word 'purpose' elicits a degree of unease and confusion because of its connection with the question of 'what God wants me to do'. Let me state at the outset that it is not my concern to deal with the specific issue of guidance in these pages; you will find no practical tips on how to 'hear the voice of God'. Instead, my concern is with the bigger picture, the context in which God has placed us and in which He is calling us to serve. My hope is that, through exploring Paul's second letter to Timothy, we can open ourselves up to a new way of seeing that is more consonant with the biblical vision of what our lives are about and less tainted by our own preconceived ideas. By first understanding the key elements of God's broad purpose for our lives we become better prepared to discern the particular ways in which He is calling us to serve. I therefore suggest three of the broad strokes that blend together in making up the big picture of the purposes of God.

1. God's purposes are accomplished in the power of the Spirit

The typical local church has been likened to a football match in which 22,000 people desperately in need of exercise watch 22 people running around a pitch desperately in need of a rest! [6] In a large number of churches, even in those that pay lip service to the values of 'lay ministry' or 'team ministry', it is not uncommon to find a small, select band of individuals taking responsibility for the larger part of the work, while their co-workers settle comfortably into their roles as side-line spectators. In Boreham's words they are 'languidly passive', reluctant to exercise their gifting in the life of the Body.

For Paul it was inconceivable that Timothy should be allowed to backslide into passivity. The apostle's first appeal is also his most important because, as we shall see, it provides the ground on which Timothy may be assured of fulfilling every further obligation that is set before him: 'I remind you to fan into flame the gift of God, which is in you through the laying on of my hands' (v.6). In spite of Timothy's irrefutable qualities as a man of spiritual maturity and 'sincere faith' (v.5) there remains the very real danger that he may be tempted to neglect his God-given gift if the way ahead is deemed too difficult. Paul therefore calls upon his young apprentice to 'stir up that inner fire which God gave you' (Phillips).

Throughout the history of this letter many of its readers have fastened their interest on the precise identification of the grace gift (Greek, 'charisma') mentioned in verse 6. The verse is also remarkable for the discussion it has generated on the means by which one may develop one's gifting. The commentator Thomas Oden, for example, writes on the 'fan into flame' clause: 'To stir up actively is the opposite of extinguishing passively ... Gifts may become atrophied due to abuse or non-use. They await our cooperative energies to be reawakened as gifts of grace.'[7] There is much that is positive about the approach of using this verse to bring practical teaching on increasing one's effectiveness in ministry. However, that is not its purpose in the context of this chapter. Here the focus is not so much on the identity of the gift *per se* as on the source of Timothy's ministry as a whole. To this end, Paul hardly pauses for breath before attending to the origin of Timothy's gift and the life-blood of his ministry – the Person of the Spirit (v.7).

It could be said that we find two different 'motifs' in verses 6 and 7. The first is Timothy's *endowment* for ministry, the gift of God that was mediated through the laying on of hands and that equips him fully for every task set before him. The second motif is Timothy's *empowerment* for ministry, the divine enabling that makes his labour fruitful and that sustains him through the course of hardship. There is no sharp division between them. Both are inter-connected and blended manifestations of the one and the same Spirit in the life of the believer. But if we were to identify which facet of the Spirit's work is emphasised more strongly in 2 Timothy chapter 1 it would be the empowerment. Having reminded Timothy of the essential nature of the Spirit and hence the qualities He brings to bear in the life and ministry of the believer (power, love and self-discipline in contrast to timidity), Paul exhorts Timothy to enter boldly into his part in suffering for the gospel, 'by the power of God' (v.8). Having previously read in verse 7 about the 'Spirit of power' it is perhaps surprising that so many miss Paul's deliberate reference to the energising work of the Spirit he promises Timothy in verse 8. And, of course, Paul speaks from his own experience (2 Cor. 4:7; 12:9).

Further evidence in support of this view is found in verse 14 where Paul calls upon Timothy to 'guard the good deposit that was entrusted to you – guard it with the help of the Holy Spirit who lives in us'. The 'good deposit' is the gospel, the content of which Paul expounds in verses 9 and 10 and which he now commits into Timothy's hands for safekeeping. In so doing, Paul hints at a practice common in ancient society. A person going on a long journey would typically entrust his valuable goods to the care of a friend who would then be under sacred duty to 'guard the deposit' (cf.1 Tim. 6:20). In this case, the context makes it clear that to safeguard the gospel deposit does not mean Timothy is to '"sit on it", but to stay loyal to it, even to the extent of taking his share in the suffering'.[8] Timothy's greatest need is for the supernatural enabling of the Holy Spirit because it is only in the Spirit's power that he can possess the fortitude to stand firm in his allegiance to the gospel.

Paul's priority in these verses is therefore not to remind

Timothy that he possesses a gift (however encouraging that may be) but to encourage him to advance in the power of the Spirit. If we were to reduce Paul's message to Timothy to its simple essence, it is not 'fan your gift into flame because you have a great gift and a valuable ministry'. Rather, Paul is saying, 'Take heart! Fan your gift into flame because the Spirit is with you and He will sustain you.'

How much we need to hear this message today. It is the good news that in Christ we receive not only a grace that saves us but that also, through the Spirit, we receive an additional, continual ministry of grace that sustains us. As Jesus promised His disciples:

> 'I am sending you out like sheep among wolves … On my account you will be brought before governors and kings as witnesses to them and to the Gentiles. But when they arrest you, do not worry about what to say or how to say it. At that time you will be given what to say, for it will not be you speaking, but the Spirit of your Father speaking through you' (Matt. 10:16–20; cf. Mark 13:9–11; Luke 21:12–19).

Similarly, in John 15 and 16, Jesus warns His disciples that their mere identification with Him will be enough to court the hostility of the world. But He concludes with the assurance that His departure from the world will mean the arrival of the Counsellor, 'the Spirit of truth', who will act as their advocate and defend them in the face of adversity (John 14:15). The inescapable message is that as believers in Christ we, too, can trust in the help of the Spirit during times of trial. Just as we are to safeguard that which has been entrusted to our care, so the Spirit will safeguard us as the sacred possession of God (cf. Eph. 1:14).

There is no Christian believer excluded from knowing the Spirit's power in his or her experience. While there are those who worry about the perceived absence of the Holy Spirit in their lives, the apostle Paul is clear: Anyone who belongs to Christ has the Spirit of Christ (Rom. 8:9b). In the present chapter Paul makes it clear that the Spirit is not to be regarded as the private possession of Timothy alone; the Spirit is 'God's empowering presence'[9] given to all.

Are you anxious about what responding to the call of God will mean for you? Are you facing opposition or hardship? Do you recognise your frailty and your absolute need for God's power in your life? The encouragement of verse 7 is for you. By receiving and believing in the Spirit as the source and sustaining power of his ministry, Timothy is fully equipped to respond to the call of God on his life. In the same way, it is in the power of the Spirit that we are able to stand firm in our loyalty to the gospel and fulfil God's purposes for our lives.

2. God's purposes are centred on the Church

'I feel the Lord is calling me out of the church for a time.' 'I can serve God more effectively on my own.' 'I used to be part of the church but I didn't get anything out of it, so I don't go any more.'

How would Paul have responded to such comments? His writing on the Church leads us to the conclusion that his disagreement would have been emphatic. In fact, given the extraordinary passion with which Paul speaks of the people of God, it is hard to imagine him finding any point of agreement at all. It is important to ask, then, why the Church is considered by Paul to be of such prime importance.

Paul and his fellow apostles were convinced of the Church's

significance because they understood the fact that we are designed to need one another. In verse 6 Timothy is reminded that he received his gift when Paul laid hands on him. When we compare this verse with 1 Timothy 4:14 it becomes clear that this was no private incident involving Paul and Timothy alone; Timothy's equipping for service happened in a community setting through the agency of prophecy. Paul and the church elders then laid hands on Timothy in order to confirm their recognition of his gift and affirm his suitability for ministry. For us today the message is clear: it is in the context of the Christian community that gifts are bestowed by God and recognised by man, and that workers are affirmed, encouraged and released into new spheres of influence for the sake of the gospel (see, eg, Acts 1:23–26; 13:2–3; 15:2–3,22).

We are not called to 'go it alone'. Paul was probably one of the most gifted Christians in the history of the Church. He describes his own ministry as being that of a 'herald, apostle and teacher' (v.11), but we might justifiably add to that list preacher, evangelist, missionary, theologian, apologist, intercessor, author and tent-maker. Never has there been an individual so utterly equipped for autonomy, yet given the choice Paul's preference would always be to work alongside others in teams (Acts 13:1ff.; 15:40ff.; 18:18–19; 19:22, 29; 20:4ff.). In this letter Paul expresses his need for Timothy to visit him quickly because 'only Luke is with me' (4:11). Paul's desire to have others alongside him is more than a request for the encouragement of companionship or for the provision of material needs (4:13); he specifically states that he is dependent on others for the effectiveness of his ministry (4:11).

There is a further sense in which we need others whom God has gathered into His Church. We need exemplars around us.

What makes 2 Timothy such a touching epistle to read is the fact that we are beckoned to come close to Paul the man and glimpse into the deep recesses of his soul. It is a letter packed full of personal pronouns – 'I' and 'my' – for Paul is continually interspersing his fatherly advice with excerpts of personal testimony and reflections on ministry. All of this is designed to inspire and encourage the young Timothy to build into his own life that which he has seen exemplified in the life of Paul; in short, Timothy is being presented with a model to be followed. In verse 8 this theme is made explicit with the words, 'join with me …' For some time Paul and Timothy had been close companions on the road (Acts 16:1–3; 17:15; 18:5; 19:22; Rom. 16:21; 1 Cor. 4:17; 16:10–11; Phil. 1:1; 2:19–22; Col. 1:1; 1 Thess. 3:2; Philem. 1). Timothy had watched Paul working in many different contexts and had no doubt been impressed by Paul's resolute commitment to the gospel in the face of opposition and hardship. And now Paul is saying to Timothy, 'You are no longer to be on the sidelines. I am calling you to step into the thick of things. My work is to become your work; I'm handing on the baton. All that you've seen modelled in me is now to become true of your own life.'

The role models we invite into our lives say more about our priorities and aspirations than many of us would be prepared to admit. Once when I was instructed on an application form to 'name three people you look up to and explain why', my potential future employer was not setting out to glean interesting trivia for the purposes of polite dinner conversation. No, this was a probing question designed deliberately to uncover the naked truth about the kind of person I am and hope one day to be. Note that the form assumed this was an answerable question, and that out of the thousands of people I have come into contact with during my life there are at least three whom I look up to as being 'role models'. In fact, the hard thing for me was to narrow down the list to only three! Having role models is part of the human condition. We cannot choose whether or not to have models in our lives; what we can choose is the kind of people they will be.

Paul undoubtedly recognised this, and it is significant that he is for ever commending himself to others as an example to be followed (Phil. 3:17; 1 Thess. 1:6; 2 Thess. 3:9). Although we may sometimes be troubled at the starkness of Paul's language, we are not to understand this as indicative of his pride or inflated sense of self-importance. Rather, Paul possessed the realisation that we learn most about how to become great in the kingdom by watching those who naturally and consistently reflect the image of Christ in their lives. Hence Paul writes to the Corinthian believers, 'Follow my example as I follow the example of Christ' (1 Cor. 11:1). Paul knew that some of the most important things in Christianity cannot be taught, they can only be caught. You can endeavour to become an excellent disciple of Jesus Christ by applying yourself to a rigorous course of theological study but that in itself will not enable you to develop fully into the person that God has created you to be. We open ourselves up to new possibilities of growth and development by having strong role models who exemplify something of Christ's life that we long to reflect in our own. We are not to copy them parrot-fashion, but we are to watch them, learn from them, and allow them to inspire us to become everything that God has called us to be.

There is a further sense in which the Church is significant. Not only do we need one another but the world needs us, and it needs us not as isolated individuals, but as people in community who express through their relationships and the totality of their life together what the gospel is all about.

Paul brought this teaching to Timothy's church some years earlier in his letter to the Ephesians. The Church is the living, breathing actualisation of what Paul terms 'the mystery', the secret plan of God kept hidden for generations, 'that through the gospel the Gentiles are heirs together with Israel ... and sharers together in the promise in Christ Jesus' (Eph. 3:6). Through the preaching of the gospel, God has destroyed the age-old hostility that existed between Jews and Gentiles by reconciling them with one another in a single community, the Church, in which both groups now 'have access to the Father by one Spirit' (Eph. 2:18). This is what the gospel means in concrete terms. The Church is what Lesslie Newbigin terms 'the hermeneutic of the Gospel',[10] the means by which the world 'sees' the gospel in concrete form and is led to an understanding of what God has accomplished through the work of Christ. In Paul's own words, God gave him grace for the Ephesian believers precisely so they may come to view their church as the means by which 'the mystery' is made plain to all (Eph. 3:2ff.).

This is the church to which Timothy committed himself as a pastor–teacher. In this second letter to Timothy there is no indication that Paul expected his young apprentice to leave his post. In fact, his exhortations for Timothy to continue in his teaching (2:14) and ministerial duties (4:5) suggest quite the opposite. Timothy is to stand his ground because the Church remains the locus of saving grace and healing love in a broken and corrupt world.

God has not given up on His Church and neither should we. God's ministry of reconciliation continues to this day although in our contemporary age the primary need is unlikely to be the abolishment of hostility between Jew and Gentile. Today the Church communicates the transforming power of the gospel most effectively to the world through the formation of heterogeneous communities in which people of different races, languages and socio-economic status relate to one another as equals by virtue of their shared experience of salvation.

Evangelicals are notoriously poor at seeing the Church in this way. While there has never before been a time when the nature of the Church has been discussed so widely, it is also true that there remains within large parts of evangelicalism a general reluctance to give the Church any prominence in its theology. This can only serve to compound the confusion that so many Spirit-filled believers have about their calling. Until we understand the close association between the gospel proclaimed and the gospel incarnate we will not be able to understand the biblical centre of God's purposes in the world – the Church.

3. God's purposes are for the sake of the gospel

One cannot read this chapter and fail to be impressed with the high regard in which Paul holds the gospel. As the scarred, incarcerated apostle reflects again on his years in ministry and gives some consideration to what lies before his young charge, Paul's thoughts are filled with the awe-inspiring value of the gospel of grace. This is his greatest passion, his proudest boast, his most valuable treasure, and Paul knows that Timothy's one chance of success in the face of opposition is to guard the teaching entrusted to him as fiercely and as selfishly as if it were his own life. Indeed, the gospel is his life, and for this reason the apostle leads Timothy again and again to where the gospel fills his gaze. In so doing, it is as if Paul is gently and lovingly encouraging Timothy to refrain from unhealthy habits of introspection that would lead him to reflect negatively on his own abilities. Similarly, while Paul is realistic about the difficult nature of the circumstances in which Timothy is likely to find himself, he wants his apprentice to avoid needless speculation about the future. Instead, he must allow his heart to be gripped once again by the glory of the gospel, and Paul holds it up to the light like a jewel so that Timothy is able to see it sparkle in its brilliance.

In this chapter Paul variously describes the gospel as 'the pattern of sound teaching' (v.13) and 'the good deposit' (v.14) but his favourite way of acknowledging its supreme value is with the term 'life'. The gospel is 'the promise of life' that is found 'in Christ Jesus' (v.1), a life that begins the moment a person places his or her trust in the Saviour and which continues beyond the grave into eternity (v.10). This is the central claim of the gospel: it is only when we come to Jesus that we can really start to live (cf. John 10:10; 11:25; 14:6). As we shall see when we come to the third chapter of this letter, the life Jesus offers is not one of thrills and spills; instead, He initiates us into an entirely new mode of existence, one in which we become more authentically human, more truly the people that God designed us to be. As a direct consequence, the bold claim of Christianity is that outside of the gospel there can be no possibility of human beings discovering the purpose for which they were made. People may invent goals for themselves based on money, family, possessions, career or some further measure of 'success', but outside of Christ they will never know an ultimate purpose that infuses their lives with genuine meaning and orientates them towards eternal life. As Peter Meadows and Joseph Steinberg wrote on the cover of their evangelistic booklet a few years ago: 'It's one thing to have a pulse. Quite another to have a life.'[11]

But the gospel is not only the gateway to finding meaning and purpose, it actually constitutes a part of that meaning and purpose. Whatever your calling there can be no doubt that it is inseparably bound up with the gospel of Christ. We are not all called to be pioneering apostles or powerful evangelists, but we are all called to be ministers of the gospel. This is why Paul writes to the Corinthians, 'We are ... Christ's ambassadors, as though God were making his appeal through us: ... Be reconciled to God!' (2 Cor. 5:20).

At the time of writing I work full time as a secondary school science teacher. There are often times when people ask, 'Don't you feel called to the ministry?' My reply is always the same: 'I *am* in ministry!' Although my salary, my tax contributions and the bulk of my working week are tied up with my role as a teacher of science, within the purposes of God my job is honoured with a status that is altogether different. I am first and foremost a minister of the gospel and, as long as I remain in my earthly body, I will always be a minister of the gospel.

It is the same for you. Regardless of your workplace, your background or what would once have been referred to as 'your station', you are called to serve as a minister of the gospel of reconciliation. God desires to use you, in all the contexts He has placed you, to witness to the reality of His grace that is found in Jesus Christ (v.9). Whatever else may be said about God's calling on your life, it is all for the sake of the glory and fame of the gospel.

Conclusion

In this chapter my concern has been to sketch the 'big picture' in which our lives are set. As I mentioned earlier, by applying ourselves to a better understanding of this picture I believe we allow ourselves to become better tuned to knowing the will of God for our lives (cf. Rom. 12:2). I cannot know the precise nature of the calling placed on the life of each person reading these words, but the Bible leaves us in little doubt about the essential character of the purposes of God. He calls us to join Him in outworking those purposes in the world, purposes that can be accomplished only in dependency on the Spirit's power, purposes that find their centre in His gathered people, the Church, and that seek to serve the glorious gospel of Jesus Christ by making Him known. Like Timothy, we may be all too aware of our weakness and frailty as we shuffle nervously forwards. But He bids us come all the same.

CHAPTER TWO

2 TIMOTHY 2

LIVING FOR THE GOSPEL
R.T. KENDALL

CALLED TO BATTLE
ANDREW SAMPSON

2 TIMOTHY 2

¹ You then, my son, be strong in the grace that is in Christ Jesus.

² And the things you have heard me say in the presence of many witnesses entrust to reliable men who will also be qualified to teach others.

³ Endure hardship with us like a good soldier of Christ Jesus.

⁴ No-one serving as a soldier gets involved in civilian affairs – he wants to please his commanding officer.

⁵ Similarly, if anyone competes as an athlete, he does not receive the victor's crown unless he competes according to the rules.

⁶ The hardworking farmer should be the first to receive a share of the crops.

⁷ Reflect on what I am saying, for the Lord will give you insight into all this.

⁸ Remember Jesus Christ, raised from the dead, descended from David. This is my gospel,

⁹ for which I am suffering even to the point of being chained like a criminal. But God's word is not chained.

¹⁰ Therefore I endure everything for the sake of the elect, that they too may obtain the salvation that is in Christ Jesus, with eternal glory.

¹¹ Here is a trustworthy saying:
If we died with him, we will also live with him;

¹² if we endure, we will also reign with him. If we disown him, he will also disown us;

[13] if we are faithless, he will remain faithful, for he cannot disown himself.

A Workman Approved by God

[14] Keep reminding them of these things. Warn them before God against quarrelling about words; it is of no value, and only ruins those who listen.

[15] Do your best to present yourself to God as one approved, a workman who does not need to be ashamed and who correctly handles the word of truth.

[16] Avoid godless chatter, because those who indulge in it will become more and more ungodly.

[17] Their teaching will spread like gangrene. Among them are Hymenaeus and Philetus,

[18] who have wandered away from the truth. They say that the resurrection has already taken place, and they destroy the faith of some.

[19] Nevertheless, God's solid foundation stands firm, sealed with this inscription: "The Lord knows those who are his," and, "Everyone who confesses the name of the Lord must turn away from wickedness."

[20] In a large house there are articles not only of gold and silver, but also of wood and clay; some are for noble purposes and some for ignoble.

[21] If a man cleanses himself from the latter, he will be an instrument for noble purposes, made holy, useful to the Master and prepared to do any good work.

[22] Flee the evil desires of youth, and pursue righteousness, faith, love and peace, along with those who call on the Lord out of a pure heart.

[23] Don't have anything to do with foolish and stupid arguments,

because you know they produce quarrels.

²⁴ And the Lord's servant must not quarrel; instead, he must be kind to everyone, able to teach, not resentful.

²⁵ Those who oppose him he must gently instruct, in the hope that God will grant them repentance leading them to a knowledge of the truth,

²⁶ and that they will come to their senses and escape from the trap of the devil, who has taken them captive to do his will.

LIVING FOR THE GOSPEL

R.T. KENDALL ON 2 TIMOTHY 2

The second chapter of 2 Timothy is about participation in the gospel, being wholeheartedly in the service of the King of kings. This chapter is very important to me. Over 40 years ago, back in 1962, I accepted a call to be the pastor of a little church in Ohio, USA, and God used 2 Timothy 2 to confirm my calling to preach His unchanging Word. I felt led to read all the way through Paul's last letter one evening, imagining that the apostle was talking to me. In those days I was using the Authorised Version and I was gripped by verse 4 of chapter 2: 'No man that warreth entangleth himself with the affairs of this life.'

That verse changed my life. It made me see the folly of debt, because getting into financial trouble entangles you with the affairs of this life. Not only that, God was showing me the folly of doing anything in my life other than preaching. It has not always been possible to do so full-time and there was a period when I had to sell vacuum cleaners to make a living. But the point is that when I read 2 Timothy 2:4 all those years ago it made me see that I must live within my own anointing.

'This is my gospel' (v.8)

Since retirement God has given me a ministry to Middle Eastern leaders and I keep saying to them: 'Look, I come as a follower of Jesus. I am not a politician – I am a theologian, I am man of prayer.' They try to get me into discussing politics but

I say, 'No, it's about Jesus. If you don't want me like that I will not come back.' We have got to live within His calling, which is why Paul says in verse 4 of this chapter, 'No-one serving as a soldier gets involved in civilian affairs – he wants to please his commanding officer.' It is one thing to say you believe the gospel, but another to partake of it, to give it everything you've got so that it's all you live for.

A friend once challenged me: 'RT, how far are you willing to go in your commitment to Jesus Christ?' I thought, 'How dare he ask me that – me, the minister at Westminster Chapel!' But that was exactly what I needed. What about you? How far are you willing to go for Jesus? What Paul is writing about in this chapter is the sharing of the gospel – passing on what we have received: 'And the things you have heard me say in the presence of many witnesses entrust to reliable men who will also be qualified to teach others' (v.2). You reach people who will reach people who will reach people – and it begins with you being a soul winner.

Have you personally led another person to Jesus Christ? When I first came to Westminster Chapel I asked, 'How many of you here have never led a soul to Christ?' A man sitting in the sixth row later admitted, 'That shook me rigid. Here I am, 60 years old. I have been a Christian since I was a boy and I realised I had never led anyone to Christ.' A few years later we started a ministry out on the streets called Pilot Lights, which was still going on after I left. One of the first team members was that same man. I know that he has led over 300 people to Jesus since then.

In 2 Timothy 1 we saw how our anointing increases through suffering. In chapter 2 Paul writes about another way: through passing on to others what we have learned. He tells Philemon in verse 6 of that little letter: 'I pray that you may be active in sharing your faith, *so that you will have a full understanding of every good thing we have in Christ*' (my italics). Do want an increase in your anointing? Dignify any suffering He gives you and become a soul winner. Lead people to Jesus! This is what Paul is saying: pass on what you have received.

Some of those you share with will become soul winners, leaders and evangelists. James Kennedy, the architect of Evangelism Explosion, said that it is better to train a person to be a soul winner than it is simply to lead a person to Christ, because if you train a person to be a soul winner there will be hundreds converted instead of one person. So be on the lookout for potential soul winners and teachers.

'Be strong' (v.1)

The writer to the Hebrews complained that although the believers he was addressing ought to be teachers by now they still needed to be taught the 'elementary truths of God's word all over again. You need milk, not solid food!' (Heb. 5:12–13). They were still infants, unable to absorb teaching on righteousness. That's a really serious problem, because the next chapter of Hebrews, which the Methodist commentator Adam Clarke has called the most difficult passage in the New Testament, warns of reaching the place where you cannot be renewed again.

It is impossible for those who have once been enlightened, who have tasted the heavenly gift, who have shared in the Holy Spirit, who have tasted the goodness of the word of God and the powers of the coming age, if they fall away, to be brought back to repentance, because to their loss they are crucifying the Son of God all over again and subjecting him to public disgrace. (Heb. 6:4–6)

This has been a theological battleground for Arminians and Calvinists. Calvinists say you can't fall away; Hebrews 6 says you can. Arminians teach that if you do fall away you can get it back; Hebrews 6 says you can't. What does it mean? It is referring to Christians who cannot be brought back to repentance because they've become stone deaf to the Holy Spirit. By stating that believers ought to have become teachers rather than still taking in milk, the writer to the Hebrews was saying that they had become dull of hearing – 'slow to learn' (Heb. 5:11). The translation from the Greek is literally 'become hard of hearing'.

My wife, Louise, started a ministry to the deaf at Westminster Chapel and we learned a bit about deafness. Unless it is caused by an accident, deafness comes in stages. The first stage is when you find yourself cupping your ear and asking for something to be repeated. The next stage is getting a hearing aid, then a stronger one, following by an even stronger instrument. The worst scenario is what experts call profoundly deaf or, as we sometimes say, stone deaf, when you can't hear anything.

The writer to the Hebrews is warning of the danger of falling away so far that you don't hear God speak any more – where it is impossible to be brought back to repentance. In that state you cannot be changed from glory to glory. Paul is saying this to Timothy.

You cannot get away from the theme of suffering for the gospel in 2 Timothy. It's in every chapter. Paul's opening statement in chapter 2 is: 'Be strong in the grace that is in Christ Jesus.' How do we become strong? Basically through three things:

1. Time spent in prayer.
2. Time spent in reading the Bible.
3. Time spent in listening to good teaching.

How much do you pray? Church leaders, how much do you spend time alone with God every day? Would you be happy for your church members to know the answer to that question? A survey of ministers and church leaders was taken on both sides of the Atlantic on how much they pray. It was found that the average was four minutes each day! And we wonder why much of the Church is powerless! Compare this to an entry in Martin Luther's Journal: 'I have a very busy day today. Must spend not two hours, but three in prayer.' The leader of the Reformation reckoned that the busier the day the more time he needed to be with God. John Wesley would not think of going out into the day without two hours on his knees from 4am to 6am. Sadly, there aren't many Wesleys or Luthers today.

How much do you read your Bible? Do you have a Scripture reading plan? How well do you know God's Word? How important is Bible teaching to you? It's part of suffering because it is sacrifice. It's a lot easier to watch your favourite TV programmes than to read the Bible; to peruse your daily newspaper than to pray. But Paul commands us to be strong in God's grace. We're living at a time when we need to do this more than ever. Children spell love T.I.M.E. It's not what you buy them at Christmas but how long you spend with them. And time seeking His face is how God expects us to express our love for Him.

Paul writes about enduring hardship, being disciplined and facing things so that when trial comes we are not going to panic. Spending time with Him will help us not to be shaken when the crisis comes. It will help us deal with injustice, overcome the disappointment of unanswered prayer, the shock of friends letting us down. Paul says in verse 10, 'I endure everything for the sake of the elect.' He was absolutely committed to the proclamation of the gospel. Having experienced its life-changing work, all he wanted was for others to experience it too. That's what he was getting at in verse 6: 'The hardworking farmer should be the first to receive a share of the crops.' He means that we cannot pass on what we don't have or have not experienced for ourselves.

When we started Evangelism Explosion in Westminster Chapel – in my opinion the best soul-winning plan I have come across – among those who enrolled was one of our doctors. After the fourth week she realised that she herself had not even been converted. Had she then not been converted herself she would not have been able to fulfil the aim of the course, which was to lead other people to salvation. Like the farmer, she had to receive the first share of the 'crop'.

How real is God to you? How important is the gospel? Do you realise what happens to people when they die not saved? Do you realise that the issue is heaven or hell? Some people say they believe in heaven but not hell. But if there is no hell there is no heaven. The Bible, however, teaches that there is both, which is why Paul writes in verse 15 of our passage about labouring to please God: 'Do your best to present yourself to God as one approved.' The Authorised Version puts it, 'Study to show thyself approved unto God.'

There is no greater or higher learning than knowing God and the Bible. The motto of Oxford University is 'The Lord is my Light'. It's taken from Psalm 27 verse 1, because when Oxford was founded back in the thirteenth century theology was king. The best minds wanted to learn it. Sadly, the top students today choose physics, medicine and law. We should pray that the day will come when there will be such a love of God and theology that all this can be reversed, and people see that there is no higher learning than getting to know God and His Word. 'No eye has seen, no ear has heard, no mind has conceived what God has prepared for those who love him' (1 Cor. 2:9). What's the purpose of all this? That you will be one who 'correctly handles the word of truth', as verse 15 puts it. The Authorised Version translates it, 'rightly dividing the word of truth'.

Why is this necessary? Because some truths are more important than others. Some sins are worse than others. Some Scripture verses are more difficult than others. So with this in mind Paul says in verse 19, 'The Lord knows those who are his.' It's a seal of the gospel. John Calvin called it 'the inner testimony of the Spirit'. It's the way you know the Bible is the Word of God. Some think the only way you can know the Bible is the Word of God is through archaeological study or the testimony of great men who have said what the Bible has meant to them. But the only one way to know and never doubt is the inner testimony of the Holy Spirit. This is the way we come into assurance of salvation, to know we are saved. Paul gives us what I would call the *Ordo Salutus* – the order of salvation. He says in verse 19, 'Everyone who confesses the name of the Lord must turn away from wickedness.'

Note the order. We don't turn away from wickedness and then confess the name of the Lord, because if we do it that way we will never know when we are finally qualified to confess His name. We begin by confessing Him as Lord and Saviour and then we repent of our sins – 'turn away from wickedness'. If you get the cart before the horse you will be like so many Christians who are not sure whether they are saved because they were taught that they couldn't know they're saved until they repent of every known sin. A long time later they think, 'Oh, here's one I haven't repented of, so I haven't been saved for the past

20 years after all.' But the truth is we are saved when we trust what Jesus did for us on the cross and confess Him as Lord and Saviour. Then God puts you on your honour to live a holy life; you're under a covenant.

'Pursue righteousness' (v.22)

Paul winds up 2 Timothy 2 by writing about the servants of the gospel. 'In a large house there are articles not only of gold and silver, but also of wood and clay; some are for noble purposes and some for ignoble. If a man cleanses himself from the latter, he will be an instrument for noble purposes, made holy, useful to the Master and prepared to do any good work' (vv.20–21). Get acquainted with the kind of person God uses and the kind of people you need to keep company with. 'Flee the evil desires of youth, and pursue righteousness, faith, love and peace, along with those who call on the Lord out of a pure heart' (v.22).

Make friends with those who love God, who show by their lives the kind of teaching we need to focus on. The apostle continues his teaching about the kind of attitude and temperament we must develop by saying, 'Don't have anything to do with foolish and stupid arguments, because you know they produce quarrels. And the Lord's servant must not quarrel; instead, he must be kind to everyone, able to teach, not resentful' (vv.23–24). Then in verses 25–26 he shows us the kind of graciousness we need to develop: we need to gently instruct those who oppose us 'in the hope that God will grant them repentance leading them to a knowledge of the truth, and that they will come to their senses and escape from the trap of the devil, who has taken them captive to do his will'. It's an inescapable fact that if you're in the ministry there will be those who will oppose you, so we have to adopt the attitude that

Paul says is the key to bringing change in their lives: gentleness in our dealings with them.

A Christian can fall into the devil's trap by being asleep spiritually. When we are asleep, we don't know we are asleep until we wake up, and then we think, 'I can't believe I was asleep.' We can be spiritually asleep and then wake up wondering, 'What has been wrong with me?' When we are asleep we dream of doing things we wouldn't do while we are awake. When we are spiritually asleep we tiptoe into the world and do things we once said we would never do. When the alarm sounds, we are unwilling to rouse from our slumbers and become unteachable. Pray that God will reach us before we become like those in Hebrews 6 who were stone deaf to the Spirit and could no longer hear God speak.

CALLED TO BATTLE

ANDREW SAMPSON ON 2 TIMOTHY 2

In his book, *The Forest People*, the late British anthropologist Colin Turnbull tells the story of how he lived among the Mbuti pygmies of the Ituri Forest, situated in the northeast corner of the Congo. One day Turnbull took a pygmy friend named Kenge out of the forest for the first time in his life and the two climbed a mountain together. Looking out over the vastness of the plains below Kenge spotted some buffalo grazing in the distance and, turning to his companion, asked, 'What insects are those?' 'At first,' writes Turnbull, 'I hardly understood, then I realised that in the forest vision is so limited that there is no great need to make an automatic allowance for distance when judging size. Out here in the plains, Kenge was looking for the first time over apparently unending miles of unfamiliar grasslands, with not a tree worth the name to give him any basis for comparison … When I told Kenge that the insects were buffalo, he roared with laughter and told me not to tell such stupid lies.'[1]

How important it is to ensure that we have a true perspective! In Chapter 1 I suggested that if we are to understand correctly God's purposes for us as individuals we first need to view our lives in the context of God's purposes for His people in general. We need to avoid narrowing our focus so we see only the humdrum things of our everyday lives and so miss the big picture of what God desires to accomplish in and through us. By focusing our eyes anew and training them to take in a broad perspective, each aspect of our lives will be viewed in a new light and brought more easily into alignment with the purposes of God. At present I believe there is a crying need for Christians to assess and refine their vision in precisely this way. We do not lack the motivation and zeal for the Lord's work; what we lack is a focus and a direction in which to channel our energies constructively. As a result, our churches are often full of busybodies who achieve little that is of any consequence because we do not know what we are living for. God's remedy is to provide for us, in His Word, the big picture that helps us make sense of our lives and guards our focus from being hijacked by purely trivial and superficial matters.

In verse 10 of chapter 2, Paul once again opens up the 'big picture' that dictates his life's purpose and informs everything in which he is involved. All that he does and all that he has ever set out to do is deemed worthwhile to the extent that it aligns with this supreme goal. He writes, 'I endure everything for the sake of the elect [ie those whom God chooses], that they too may obtain the salvation that is in Christ Jesus, with eternal glory.' This, in a single sentence, is what Paul's life is all about. He is on a rescue mission, and now he writes so that Timothy may view his life in the same way, sharing Paul's passion to see men and women come under the sound of the gospel and receive the salvation that comes through belief in Christ.

It will not be easy. The mention of endurance in verse 10 is an indication that Paul's intimate acquaintance with opposition and hardship leads him to expect Timothy to find his own experience of ministry equally tough. The present chapter is therefore Paul's warning to Timothy of impending danger, and a description of the specific perils that threaten to ruin his effectiveness in ministry and divert him from his God-given course.

In providing Timothy with this warning, Paul departs from his standard practice of setting out a single, cogent argument. Instead, I see in this chapter three distinct themes that Paul visits and revisits at different times and in different ways. These are what I term 'erroneous ideas and wordplay,' second, evil desires, and finally, hardship.

1. Erroneous ideas and wordplay

This, the first of the three themes, comes to prominence in the second half of the chapter, where Paul issues a firm warning about those who bring false teaching into the Church. In chapter 1, we heard how key church figures had begun to desert Paul and the gospel he stood for, as a result of which the church in Ephesus was coming under the influence of people whose ideas owed more to whim and fancy than to divine revelation. In the present chapter, Paul describes them variously as people who engage in 'quarrelling about words' (v.14), 'godless chatter' (v.16) and 'foolish and stupid [or unlearned] arguments' (v.23). Who these people are and where their ideas come from is debatable, and as the biblical record gives us relatively little to go on, any answer will be based in large part on speculation. To my mind, at least, it seems that we would be ill advised to go any further than John Calvin who, in 1548, summed up the key characteristic of these false teachers with the phrase 'quarrelsome speculation'.[2] My own phrase, 'erroneous ideas and wordplay', seeks to capture the same idea of subversive theology being brought together with pointless and contentious debate. From this chapter it becomes clear that one of Paul's overriding concerns is that Timothy should shun those who delight in entering profitless and heated controversies that fail to align with the plumb-line of Scripture.

In our contemporary age individuals given over to error and

wordplay are likely to appear in at least two different guises. First, they come to us in the form of people who neglect the central thrust of God's Word by focusing on trivialities. Here is the 'one issue Christian' who, through selective reading, or the mishandling of the Word, or just plain ignorance, manages to make a peripheral issue central and the hub of his missionary endeavour. I once knew a dear Christian brother who always managed to steer a conversation round to what he considered to be the burning theological issue of the moment – the evil of the European Union. The fact that much of his opinion was based on information gleaned from the pages of the tabloids rather than the Bible seemed immaterial to him; as far as he was concerned, he had been given a divine mandate to press the importance of this issue on the Church and to bring others round to his way of thinking.

There are plenty of other issues that lend themselves to taking on undue significance in the hearts and minds of believers. Major battles have been fought in churches over issues like water baptism, speaking in tongues, creation and evolution, spiritual warfare and the merits of a particular Bible translation. These issues and the debates that ensue may be important in themselves, but when they become the main thing they can quite literally drive Christians to distraction. All too often such controversies generate more heat than light because one side is unable to entertain the idea that anything can be learned from the position of the other. Moreover, they threaten to undermine our missionary effectiveness in the world, because the Church quickly becomes known more for its inward bickering than for its commitment to the outward thrust of the gospel.

We also need to beware of those who seek to 'improve' God's Word by blending it with fashionable ideas. In verse 18 Paul warns Timothy about two men named Hymenaeus and Philetus 'who have wandered away from the truth' by saying that 'the resurrection has already taken place'. It is important to note that the error of these men does not lie in their complete rejection of biblical doctrine. Instead, starting with the truth about the resurrection, they are guilty of giving it a subtle twist to enhance its plausibility and acceptability to their own crooked way of thinking. This is no isolated incident. A casual glance at any period of church history shows that people have always sought to 'improve' the foundational truths of God's Word through the removal of unpalatable truth or the addition of new insight. Sometimes the reinterpretation of the text has been so complete that the message of the gospel has been all but lost. At other times, a second text has been claimed to offer a new source of revelation that discloses the key to unlocking the Bible's 'true' meaning. The consequence of both is the same: men and women are led away from the message of salvation that is accomplished by the cross of Christ and effected through the agency of the Spirit. Paul knew only too well that the ingenuity of human reason can lead to a denial of the wisdom of God (1 Cor. 1:18–2:16).

In our own day it is perhaps most common for the error of Hymenaeus and Philetus to be found among those who seek to 'demythologise' the Bible. Note again that I am not talking about those who reject the Scriptures outright. They may be very sincere people who acknowledge the significance of the Bible and even recognise it as being in some sense inspired. Where the demythologisers go astray, however, is in affording their human reason a higher authority than the postulates of Scripture. They often identify the supernatural elements of Scripture as mere by-products of the Bible being written in a less sophisticated, non-scientific age, and regard these elements as incidental to what the original authors were actually trying to convey. They devote themselves to uncovering the message of the Scriptures with the aid of language and categories totally alien to the original authors. Sometimes this is taken to such an extent that one cannot help thinking that the scholar is claiming to know the thoughts of the author better than the author himself. Who, we must ask, is the one who is divinely inspired?

The demythologisers are largely to blame for the fact that, in our contemporary culture, the Bible is accepted as one of a number of religious texts that serve no greater purpose than to inspire us to love our neighbour. Never has the Bible been so roundly accepted and its fundamental message so misunderstood. The fanciful ideas spouted forth by the demythologisers are persuasive because they resonate with the language and thought forms of our age; indeed, this is what inspired them in the first place. There are many inside and outside the Church who have already allowed their confidence in the Scriptures to become undermined by the arguments of modern scholarship. As a result their trust in the power of the gospel has been all but lost and they are robbed of playing their part in the purposes of God. It is sobering to realise that, in Paul's view, quarrelling about words is not only profitless, it 'ruins those who listen' (v.14) and destroys people's faith (v.18b). The word translated 'ruins' is, in the original Greek, '*katastrophē*,' and it is therefore no exaggeration to say that the godless practices of the error-mongers, if permitted or participated in by members of the Church, have consequences that are quite literally catastrophic. Paul emphasises the devastating effect of these practices by likening them to a gangrene, which, as it spreads through the Body of Christ, results in spiritual death and decomposition wherever it goes (v.17).

So Paul is at pains to make sure that Timothy does not allow himself to get caught up in these things. He issues him with two commands, both designed to keep him on the straight and narrow without being distracted from his God-given purpose. In the first place, Timothy is to turn away and dissociate himself from all idle chatter that refuses to align itself with scriptural principles (vv.16, 23). Refusing to enter into spurious debate and speculation will safeguard Timothy's own fitness for service, but there remains the bigger question of how false teaching can be rooted out altogether for the sake of the health of the Church. The second part of Timothy's response is therefore to be an offensive as well as a defensive measure. 'Do your best,' writes Paul, 'to present yourself to God as ... a workman ... who correctly handles the word of truth' (v.15). John Stott points out that the verb translated here as 'correctly handles' means literally 'to cut straight' in the manner of building a straight road or driving a straight furrow.[3] Timothy must refuse to allow his understanding and application of the Word to be determined by the contours of the prevailing ideological landscape. He must be quick to recognise and guard against the postulates of fashionable thinking that would divert him from his course and damage the Church. Instead, he is called to remain true to the 'pattern of sound teaching' (1:13) in the knowledge that, while his faithfulness in this matter will not court him the favour of sinful man, it is certain to bring him the favour that really counts – approval in the eyes of God (v.15a).

When reading this command of Paul to Timothy, one cannot help wondering about the extent to which Christians today are equipped for the correct handling of the Word. Across large parts of the Church there is evidence of a worrying lack of expertise with which Christians expound and apply biblical truth. It is not uncommon for large parts of the Bible, particularly from the Old Testament, to be viewed as more or less 'out of bounds', with many believers confessing that they lack the knowledge or the confidence to access text written in a time and culture so far removed from our own. When the Bible is read, the focus is often restricted to a spattering of favourite verses with little thought to how they find their context and meaning within the grand narrative of Scripture. It is not helped by the fact that many Christians, rightly concerned about the damaging influences of liberal thought on biblical scholarship, now frown on the academic study of theology altogether. A few years ago I heard a talk from a well-known Christian speaker who began by ridiculing and denouncing the merits of theological study, and then announced proudly, 'I do not have a degree in a school of theology, I have a degree in the school of *experience*.' There is, of course, much wisdom to be gained from being attentive to what God says through the lessons of experience, but this in itself is not enough to strengthen the Church and edify the saints. Nor can experience alone help us to effectively resist the advances of erroneous doctrine.

Paul identifies this final objective as a key feature of Timothy's ministerial role in verse 25. Here he tells Timothy not only what he must do but how he is to do it: with an attitude of gentleness. The apologist Ravi Zacharias, himself no stranger to standing up to those who oppose biblical truth, is fond of quoting the adage, 'Those who throw mud not only get their hands dirty, they also lose the ground they are standing on.' In contrast to the squabbling and quarrelling that characterises the internal debate of the error-mongers, Timothy's dialogue with them is to be marked by kindness, calmness and respect. But this is not to make him a soft touch: gentleness of attitude is not be confused with softness of character. Timothy is to enter into controversy in order to teach (v.24b), to remain unmoved in his adherence to the truth and in his resolve to bring others to a right understanding of the gospel.

The seriousness of Paul's charge to Timothy is underlined by his mention of Satan in verse 26 – the only occasion the devil appears in this letter. Timothy cannot afford to become lazy and undisciplined in his study of the Word, nor can he permit himself to flirt with the popular ideas and persuasive arguments of the false teachers. Although the practices of those committed to erroneous ideas and wordplay may, at times, seem harmless enough, Paul pulls back the curtain to reveal a dangerous and powerful enemy who is using them to achieve his evil ends. Satan, it should be remembered, often 'masquerades as an angel of light' (2 Cor. 11:14). Timothy must not allow his commitment to the Word of God to be shaken by false teaching, nor must he give in to compromise. There is a long and bitter battle ahead.

2. Evil desires

The second threat to Timothy fulfilling his divine mandate is described in verse 22 as the 'evil desires of youth'. Here it becomes clear that, for all Paul's talk elsewhere about the Christian being 'dead to sin' and free from its domination (Rom. 6), he remains a realist in his view that sin has not entirely lost its power in the mind and heart of the believer. Timothy no longer belongs to his old master, the sinful nature, but Paul acknowledges he can still be influenced by it. In the words of John Wesley, 'sin does not *reign,* but it does remain'.[4] Paul therefore charges Timothy with the responsibility of ensuring that he does not endanger the effectiveness of his ministry by indulging his sinful nature.

No doubt Timothy would have known already about the

importance of maintaining a clear conscience by refusing to succumb to temptation. Paul's exhortation therefore goes beyond telling him merely to ensure that he does not give in to it; rather, Timothy's response to temptation is to actively run away from it in hot pursuit of 'righteousness, faith, love and peace' (v.22). In this way Timothy is to be like Joseph, another young man from the pages of the Bible who, when confronted by the temptation of a woman's advances, did not wait to see if he could stand up under it. Instead, we are told that Joseph 'ran out of the house', leaving his cloak in her hand but his honour firmly intact (Gen. 39:12). It is not unreasonable to suppose that in behaving this way in private, Joseph proved himself to God as someone who could be trusted with significant leadership responsibility in public. Hence 'the LORD was with Joseph and gave him success in whatever he did' (Gen. 39:23), duly resulting in his exaltation as Pharaoh's number two (Gen. 41:43) and the saviour of Egypt (Gen. 41:53–57).

If we could see the premium that God places on the quality of character in his servants we would be considerably less inclined to sin. David writes in the book of Psalms, 'Who may ascend the hill of the LORD? Who may stand in his holy place?' He then answers, 'He who has clean hands and pure heart, who does not lift up his soul to an idol or swear by what is false' (Psa. 24:3–4). The promise of communion with God and the experience of His blessing are contingent on the pursuit of holiness in the life of the believer. If this is true for believers in general, it is all the more so for those called to positions of leadership or other roles of responsibility. David was keenly aware from his own experience of the importance of maintaining purity of heart and integrity of character (2 Sam. 12:13–14; Psa. 51); indeed, it was on this basis that he was chosen by God as Israel's king in the first place (1 Sam. 16:7).

In verses 20 and 21 Paul uses the metaphor of household items to make this very point. The issue is the kind of person that God chooses to use in His service as 'an instrument for noble purposes' (v.21). In the Church, the house of God, there are both valuable items used for 'noble purposes' and invaluable items used for purposes described as 'ignoble'. Most commentators are agreed that Paul is here contrasting the worthlessness of the peddlers of false ideas discussed in the previous section with the intrinsic worth of those who adhere to sound doctrine. But if the latter, noble members are to be truly effective in their Master's service, they must first ensure that their lives are untainted by the evil influences of the former. Consequently there is the requirement of regular cleansing, for 'everyone who confesses the name of the Lord must turn away from wickedness' (v.19b). Paul is emphasising the point that if Timothy is to be effective in ministry, the gifting which is so evident in his life is not enough; he must also ensure that he remains among those who 'call on the Lord out of a pure heart' (v.22b). As J.I. Packer writes in *A Passion for Holiness*:

> Ministry blossoms naturally in holy lives. In effective ministry, God's power is channelled through God's servants into areas of human need. A saintly person of limited gifts is always likely to channel more of it than would a person who was more gifted but less godly. So God wants us all to seek holiness and usefulness together, and the former partly at least for the sake of the latter.[5]

One can hardly stress this point enough. In the same book,

Packer quotes the great Scottish preacher Robert Murray McCheyne as saying, 'My people's greatest need is my personal holiness.'[6] The commentator Thomas Oden, writing about verses 20 and 21, goes even further in relating the Christian leader's purity of heart to the Church's hope for renewal and revitalisation:

> There will be no rebirth of Christianity in the modern world without a rebirth of ministry, and there will be no rebirth of ministry without a purification, a cleansing which we have not even begun to see.[7]

A few years ago the Lord challenged me on this point with respect to my own life and ministry by pointing me towards the advice given to the young man in Proverbs 4:23: 'Above all else, guard your heart, for it is the wellspring of life.' Any young man striving to follow Christ knows only too well how easy it is for the heart to become polluted with sin and to feel that the totality of his Christian life has become stagnant and staid as a result. How, then, is the wellspring of the heart to be kept free from the damaging effects of pollution? The answer to this question is important not only for the spiritual wellbeing of the person concerned but, as we have seen, for the effectiveness of his or her ministry in the service of God. It is, in fact, the subject of the second of Paul's metaphors from chapter 2, the image of the athlete in verse 5.[8] Here, Timothy is told that if he is to know success in Christian life and ministry he must run the race 'according to the rules'. Paul's words here are strongly reminiscent of what he has already written some years earlier, in his first letter to the Corinthians:

Everyone who competes in the games goes into strict training … I do not run like a man running aimlessly; I do not fight like a man beating the air. No, I beat my body and make it my slave so that after I have preached to others, I myself will not be disqualified for the prize. (1 Cor. 9:25–27)

Paul speaks here of victory being incumbent on firm discipline. An Olympic champion does not prepare for the Games by succumbing to self-indulgence or the pressures placed upon him by those who are not in training. No, every desire that threatens to deteriorate his performance must be curbed, every passion that threatens to distract him from his goal must be quashed. In the same way, Timothy is to incorporate discipline in his life as part of his training for fruitfulness and godliness (cf. 1 Tim. 4:7b–8), for it is well said no one can master others until he has first learned to master himself.

We have seen that Timothy's mission is placed under pressure from three different sources, a triad of enemies that threatens to divert him from his course and compel him to forfeit his calling. First, there are the evil desires that stem from his sinful nature and serve to lean him towards impurity and ungodliness. Second, there are the fashionable ideas and arguments inspired by the kind of worldly thinking that elevates human reason over and above the revelation that comes from God, and that, third, owes its ultimate origin to the will of the devil. Here, then, are the dangers to be watched for: the flesh, the world and the devil, or, in the words of Arthur Wallis, the '*internal* enemy', the '*external* enemy', and the '*infernal* enemy'.[9] Timothy finds himself in a battle, and in any battle a soldier must attend to his fitness and preparedness with the utmost diligence.

In the classic British comedy series *Dad's Army*, an unlikely band of men is trained for their part in World War Two by the home guard platoon leader, Captain Mainwaring. While the British troops are engaged in the ferocity of battle overseas, Mainwaring has the unenviable task of training his platoon in the relatively comfortable surroundings of wartime England. At times he finds it practically impossible to withhold his frustration at all the complacency he sees around him, and numerous people throughout the series find themselves at the receiving end of his blast: 'There is a war on, you know!' The same is also true of the context in which we live our lives, whether we perceive it or not. We, like Timothy, are called to be aware of the battle that rages for our hearts and minds and to ensure that we are adequately prepared to enter into the fray. In any battle there will be trials, hardships and sufferings, and this brings us to the final major threat that Paul identifies in this chapter.

3. Hardship

It is said that one of the defining characteristics of being British is the strength of character popularly described as the 'stiff upper lip', Looking back over the history of our nation, this was perhaps never more evident than during the Blitz of 1940–41. Astonishingly, even as the bombs were falling on the city of London, one of its golf clubs, based in Richmond, declared 'business as usual' with the introduction of these temporary rules:

> In competition, during gunfire or while bombs are falling, players may take cover without penalty for ceasing play. The positions of known delayed-action bombs are marked by red flags at a reasonably, but not guaranteed, safe distance therefrom ... A ball moved by enemy action may be replaced,

or, if lost or destroyed, a ball may be dropped not nearer the hole without a penalty. A player whose stroke is affected by the simultaneous explosion of a bomb may play another ball from the same place. Penalty, one stroke.[10]

I am writing these words just one week after the 7 July 2005 bomb attacks in London, the first ever suicide attacks to be carried out on British soil. Once again, the people of London are being roundly praised for their gritty resolve to continue calmly and confidently with their lives. They share the determination of their World War Two forbears not to allow the enemy to get the better of them by giving in to fear.

Paul writes that something of the same spirit is to characterise the life of Timothy. He, too, will experience a welter of heavy blows from the opposition, yet he must not allow his course to be altered, nor must he allow his resolve to be dampened. This anticipates much of the discussion to be developed in chapter 3, and consequently I here restrict my attention to two further metaphors that Paul uses in the present chapter.

The first of these metaphors is found in verse 3 where Paul writes, 'Endure hardship with us like a good soldier of Christ Jesus.' The image of the soldier is one of Paul's favourite vehicles for explaining the character of the Christian life (1 Cor. 9:7; 2 Cor. 6:7; 10:3–5; Eph. 6:11–18). He calls two of his close associates 'fellow-soldiers' (Phil. 2:25; Philem. 2) and, in his first letter, he issues Timothy a cry to throw himself into battle (1 Tim. 1:18; 6:12). This, however, is the first time Paul spells it out clearly for his young protégé. Timothy is not like a civilian in London who, through sheer bad fortune, finds himself caught up in an air raid or a terrorist attack. Rather, he serves as a soldier of Christ Jesus whose role it is – no, whose duty it is – to discount the comforts of civilian life in order to 'please his commanding officer' (v.4). Hardship is therefore a certainty, and Timothy must prepare himself for the worst so that he might have the determination to endure it.

In verse 6, however, the image changes, and Paul points Timothy to the example of a 'hardworking farmer'. The similarity Paul desires to draw between the experience of the farmer and the Lord's servant is clear: both are in the habit of giving themselves earnestly to 'diligent toil'[11] in the present so that they may be assured of receiving a rich reward in the future. Significantly, this metaphor is among those that Timothy is commanded to reflect upon (v.7a), for here we find a key incentive for his continued perseverance.

Conclusion: 'Remember Jesus Christ'

In any battle it is easy to get disheartened and discouraged, and this is as true of us now as it was of Timothy then. We may despair at the steep decline of the western Church, or our friends' lack of interest in an outreach event, or our work colleagues' rejection and ridicule of our Christian testimony. It is important, then, that we, like Timothy, keep in mind Paul's simple, three-word exhortation of verse 8. A mere three words, yet to me these are three of the most majestic and comforting words we find anywhere in the epistle: 'Remember Jesus Christ'. These words echo a phrase used by the writer to the Hebrews who similarly seeks to offer encouragement to worn down and battle-weary Christians for the way ahead. 'Let us fix our eyes on Jesus,' he declares, 'the author and perfecter of our faith, who for the joy set before him endured the cross, scorning its shame, and sat down at the right hand of the throne of God. Consider him who endured such opposition from sinful men, so that you will not grow weary and lose heart' (Heb. 12:2–3).

In verse 8 Paul speaks of two truths we are to keep in mind about Jesus. First, we are to remind ourselves that He is 'Jesus Christ, raised from the dead'. Here, the translation offered us by the New International Version is somewhat misleading, for it implies that Paul has the historic fact of the resurrection in mind. In fact, Paul does not use a past tense verb ('raised') but a passive participle, which renders the phrase in a quite different way: 'risen from the dead'. The point is not that Jesus was miraculously raised from the dead once upon a time, many years ago. Rather, Paul is saying that Christ is at this moment risen, highly exalted at the right hand of the Father in the heavenly realm, from where He exercises His lordship over the whole of His created order. He is seated on the throne, and as long as He is in possession of the power and the authority the Christian can be confident that He will build His Church, and that even 'the gates of Hades will not overcome it' (Matt. 16:18).

But there is in verse 8 a second truth about the Person of Jesus Christ. Paul seeks to emphasise not only His divine power and authority but, in speaking of His human descent, to remind us of His humanity. Here, then, is the holy mystery that Christ is 'at once complete in Godhead and complete in manhood, truly God and truly man'.[12] While Christ is a member of the triune Godhead, showing us what God is like, He took on our human likeness in order to reveal what it means to be authentically human, the people that God designed us to be. This means that when Jesus walked on the earth in submission to the will of the Father, surrendering all His ambitions and desires in order to live solely for the glory of God, He was showing us how we, too, should conduct our lives. The values by which He lived must be our values, His love must be our love, His endurance must be our endurance. To paraphrase the words of the apostle Peter, He left for us an example so that we would follow in His footsteps (1 Pet. 2:21b).

CHAPTER THREE

2 TIMOTHY 3

MAINTAINING THE PURITY OF THE
GOSPEL
R.T. KENDALL

ENDURANCE IN THE FACE OF
OPPOSITION
ANDREW SAMPSON

2 TIMOTHY 3

Godlessness in the Last Days

[1] But mark this: There will be terrible times in the last days.

[2] People will be lovers of themselves, lovers of money, boastful, proud, abusive, disobedient to their parents, ungrateful, unholy,

[3] without love, unforgiving, slanderous, without self-control, brutal, not lovers of the good,

[4] treacherous, rash, conceited, lovers of pleasure rather than lovers of God –

[5] having a form of godliness but denying its power. Have nothing to do with them.

[6] They are the kind who worm their way into homes and gain control over weak-willed women, who are loaded down with sins and are swayed by all kinds of evil desires,

[7] always learning but never able to acknowledge the truth.

[8] Just as Jannes and Jambres opposed Moses, so also these men oppose the truth – men of depraved minds, who, as far as the faith is concerned, are rejected.

[9] But they will not get very far because, as in the case of those men, their folly will be clear to everyone.

Paul's Charge to Timothy

[10] You, however, know all about my teaching, my way of life, my purpose, faith, patience, love, endurance,

[11] persecutions, sufferings – what kinds of things happened to me

in Antioch, Iconium and Lystra, the persecutions I endured. Yet the Lord rescued me from all of them.

[12] In fact, everyone who wants to live a godly life in Christ Jesus will be persecuted,

[13] while evil men and impostors will go from bad to worse, deceiving and being deceived.

[14] But as for you, continue in what you have learned and have become convinced of, because you know those from whom you learned it,

[15] and how from infancy you have known the holy Scriptures, which are able to make you wise for salvation through faith in Christ Jesus.

[16] All Scripture is God-breathed and is useful for teaching, rebuking, correcting and training in righteousness,

[17] so that the man of God may be thoroughly equipped for every good work.

MAINTAINING THE PURITY OF THE GOSPEL

R.T. KENDALL ON 2 TIMOTHY 3

It has been said that some people are made by the times and some people are made for the times. Ask yourself, as we look at this difficult chapter, which is true of you. The reason I pose this searching question is that one of the hardest things to maintain throughout the history of the Church has been the purity of the gospel. The gospel is so simple, and because it is simple people say, 'It can't be just that.' We get to heaven because Jesus died for us on the cross and we trust in what He did, not in our own deeds – however good they may be. That's it! It's good news, but the problem is that human nature doesn't take it at face value and wants to do something to earn it. Once we go down that route it ceases to be good news and we end up with a gospel of works.

'Terrible times' (v.1)

What can sometimes seem to be the minutest deviation from the gospel, innocent at first, will become, years later, gross heresy, and the gospel totally eclipsed by false teaching. If a plane that leaves John F Kennedy Airport in New York for London is just one tenth of a degree off-course 100 miles out over the Atlantic, it might be tempting to think that it's no problem. But if the pilot does not get back on course the plane will be over Spain eight hours later instead of preparing to come in to land at London Heathrow. It is vital that we, too, keep on course and maintain the purity of the gospel.

Martin Luther's realisation of justification by faith alone turned the world upside down. But 100 years later, sad to relate, the Puritans got into scholastic arguments and said, 'But how do you know you've got faith?' Luther had never found this a problem because he just trusted in what Jesus had done for him on the cross. 'Ah,' said the Puritans, 'but how do you know you are really trusting?' Soon they were in a cloud of depression, not knowing whether they were saved. We often take the purity of the gospel for granted, but 2 Timothy 3 shows how it can be undermined – and how important it is that we know what we believe.

So Paul writes in verse 1 about 'terrible times in the last days' – 'perilous times' the Authorised Version puts it. There are two issues here that we can't totally resolve. Firstly, by 'last days' does he mean the last generation of the Church or later on? Every generation of the Church has thought they were in the last days, and we tend to think so today. There is no way to prove conclusively. The other issue is whether this is a reference to society or Christendom. If it is the former it shows how bad society actually becomes where there is a deterioration of principles that once sustained it, a falling away from an element of the good.

John Calvin taught what is called common grace – 'special grace in nature' he described it. It is what keeps the world from being topsy-turvy. We have law and order – policemen, firemen, doctors, nurses and others – to maintain some degree of stability in the world. It is God's general goodness. But Paul is writing about a day coming when 'people will be lovers of themselves, lovers of money, boastful, proud, abusive, disobedient to their parents, ungrateful, unholy, without love, unforgiving, slanderous, without self-control, brutal, not lovers of the good, treacherous, rash, conceited, lovers of pleasure rather than lovers of God' (vv.2–5). Could this actually happen? Is it possible that even the good that has prevented society from being utterly evil is disappearing, or is this a description of Christendom – the Church generally?

The Church has been described as 'The Church Invisible' and the 'The Visible Church'. The Invisible describes those who are truly saved – God's elect, the regenerate. The Visible Church would be everybody around you, everybody who has been baptised and is part of the Church and society – called 'Christendom'. So Paul could be describing Christendom in the last days, when people are boastful, proud, abusive, disobedient to parents. When the nuclear family disintegrates, and there is little or no respect for parental authority and parents utterly lose control. When families disintegrate, and husbands and wives divorce and children grow up with single parents, no parents or parents who leave them to fend for themselves while they work, bereft of love and proper control. This is happening in our day.

Paul called the fifth commandment, 'Honour your father and mother' (Deut. 5:16) 'the first commandment with a promise' (Eph. 6:2–3). Would you like to live a long time? The promise of old age is for those who honour their parents. If you haven't done it lately, call your Dad and Mum and say, 'I love you.' They would love to hear that! And honour them – really honour them.

Devotion to pleasure is certainly true of today's society. This is in direct opposition to God, for it serves only to satisfy sinful desires. We are living in the 'me' generation. What's in it for me? This has crept into the Church. Much of the prosperity teaching, the 'health and wealth' gospel, encourages self-centredness.

In attempting to make the gospel relevant and attractive, the message becomes 'God wants you to be rich'. So unsaved people say, 'Well, maybe I'm interested in Christianity after all!' Its appeal is to where people are by nature.

Contrast this to Paul's statement to the church at Corinth: 'I resolved to know nothing while I was with you except Jesus Christ and him crucified' (1 Cor. 2:2). He decided, as it were, to show Christianity's worst face, to say the most offensive thing imaginable – that we are saved because someone died upon a cross. Have you any idea what a crucifixion was like in the ancient world? See Mel Gibson's film, *The Passion of the Christ*, and you will get the picture. Anybody who was crucified was the scum of the earth, and Paul is saying that this is the way we are saved! You can imagine some sophisticated believer admonishing the apostle: 'Go gently, don't bring that in too soon because they're not going to like it if you wade straight in.' But Paul went straight in with the truth. He knew that the Holy Spirit uses the purity of the gospel to save lost mankind, walking along the road to hell.

The first question of the Westminster Catechism is, 'What is the chief end of man?' Answer: 'To glorify God and to enjoy him for ever.' That means being lovers of God, not lovers of pleasure. That Paul is pointing at Christendom – the Visible Church – rather than society in general in the last days, is revealed by his statement in verse 5: 'having a form of godliness but denying its power.'

'A form of godliness' (v.5)

In the Church power should accompany the form. Some years ago an Episcopal rector in America shocked his denomination in a nationwide broadcast when he said, 'If the Holy Spirit were completely taken from the Church today, 90 per cent of the work of the Church would go right on as if nothing had happened.' This can be true of an individual believer. The Spirit can be withdrawn, we can lose the anointing and become stone deaf to the Spirit, but because of natural ability we can carry on.

The scary thing is we can even use the gifts of the Spirit – without the anointing. Not possible? It is. King Saul was on his way to kill David when he prophesied (1 Sam. 19:23–24). Does that mean he was really in touch with God? No, because earlier on it says that the Lord had left him (1 Sam. 15:26). But he prophesied. Praying in tongues, singing in tongues and speaking in tongues is no proof of spirituality. You can have the form and carry right on. You can have the Word without the Spirit. When Paul said, 'Our gospel came to you not simply with words, but also with power' (1 Thess. 1:5), he implied that it might have come in word only. I fear that in my own ministry this has too often been the case – saying the right things, or as Dr Martyn Lloyd-Jones put it, 'Perfectly orthodox, perfectly useless.'

How easy it is to have the form without the power. We think, 'Ah, this liturgy is lovely' or 'It's great to have such lively worship'. But it doesn't mean that God is in it. Talented people leading worship can hide the lack of His presence. A preacher can be a brilliant orator, enthralling his listeners, but the message may not have the anointing of the Spirit. There has been a silent divorce in the Church, generally speaking, between the Word and the Spirit. When a husband and wife divorce sometimes the children stay with the mother, sometimes with the father. In this Church divorce you have those on the Word side and those on what I would call the Spirit side.

Those on the Word side say we need to get back to the Reformation, to re-discover what Martin Luther saw; we need to get back to the God of Jonathan Edwards, to justification by faith, the sovereignty of God, earnestly contending for the faith once delivered unto the saints. Until we're back in Scripture and expository preaching, the argument goes, nothing is going to happen to honour God. There's nothing wrong with that emphasis, except that it's not enough. Those on the Spirit side say what is needed is worship, prayer, the gifts of the Spirit, signs, wonders, miracles, an enactment of the power that we saw in the book of Acts, such as when Peter's shadow resulted in people being healed. Until this happens the honour of God's name will not be restored. There's nothing wrong with this view either, but again it's not enough. What is needed at the present time is not one or the other, but both of them coming together. I believe that this combination will result in the restoration of the honour of God's name because there will not just be the form, but the power.

'Continue in what you have learned' (v.14)

After warning that a perilous time would come when there would be a form of godliness without the power, Paul then moves on to perversion of the truth and refers, I believe, especially to leaders. He says, 'They are the kind who worm their way into homes and gain control over weak-willed women' (v.6). The Roman Catholic Church in the United States was rocked by revelations of priests and even bishops abusing children, including little boys, many years previously. Celibacy, especially in the Catholic Church, can be a chosen way to honour God, but some have gone into the priesthood to do the very things that are unthinkable. Paul is warning about those who use (abuse) their positions – and they can be Protestant ministers as well as Catholic priests – to hurt and take advantage of people, especially women who may be lonely, depressed or unhappily married.

There is nothing new in this. 'Eli's sons were wicked men; they had no regard for the LORD ... This sin of the young men was very great in the LORD's sight, for they were treating the LORD's offering with contempt' (1 Sam. 2:12,17). Such people, says Paul, 'are loaded down with sins and are swayed by all kinds of evil desires'. This is why I think the apostle is not just referring to society but to those who actually profess the name of God. Paul illustrates this by naming the two men who stood against Moses (you won't find these names anywhere else in the Bible): 'Just as Jannes and Jambres opposed Moses, so also these men oppose the truth – men of depraved minds, who, as far as the faith is concerned, are rejected' (v.8). This is about lost people – those in the ministry who have never been converted.

The contrast comes in verse 10: 'You, however, know all about my teaching, my way of life, my purpose, faith, patience, love, endurance ...' What a mentor Timothy had! What kind of mentor are you? Often we are unaware that we are mentors, but there are people following our lifestyle, looking to us for example and encouragement. I'm sure I'm a mentor to some. Once in a while, someone will come up to me and say what an encouragement I have been – a pleasant surprise! Sometimes, however, we can be very much aware of being a mentor because we may have a very close relationship with someone and are helping to shape his or her life. Timothy had the honour of being mentored by Paul. I had the great privilege, for the first four years at Westminster Chapel, to have Dr Martyn-Lloyd Jones as my mentor. What an honour that was! Today mentoring is needed more than ever.

'You ... know all about my teaching ...' I love the way the Authorised Version has it: 'Thou hast fully known my doctrine.' Teaching is so important. You may prefer worship because 'teaching is so boring'. Sometimes it is, but we cannot ignore it. Jesus told the disciples when the Holy Spirit comes He 'will remind you of everything I have said to you' (John 14:26). When the disciples heard Jesus teach – the parables, the Sermon on the Mount – I'm sure they thought, 'How can we remember all this?' Not to worry, said Jesus, for when the Holy Spirit comes He will remind you what you've learned.

You may find it difficult to take things in. In that case, try memorising Scripture. It's an art that has almost perished from the earth. I spoke in a prison in the state of Idaho, USA, and there was a prisoner who had been converted and had memorised Romans chapters 4, 5 and 6. He stood up before all the other inmates and got every word right. If you're empty-headed when the Spirit comes down, how can He remind you of what you've learned when there's nothing there? But if you've taken the time to discipline yourself by meditating on and memorising Scripture, listened to good preaching and teaching, then it will come alive when the Spirit comes. That's what happened with the disciples: the Lord brought it to their attention.

You may want the laying on of hands and you may fall on the floor, but if you are empty-headed when you fall, you'll be empty-headed when you get up! It is important that something is there through learning. When Charles Spurgeon started a college in London in the nineteenth century he said, 'We will not only teach young men how to preach, we will teach them what to preach' – the purity of the gospel.

In writing about his faith, patience, love, endurance, persecutions and sufferings Paul was referring to his character and conduct as an example to follow, as Timothy well knew.

Can you commend your lifestyle to those whom you mentor? Does verse 12 grip you? 'In fact everyone who wants to live a godly life in Christ Jesus will be persecuted.' Are you godly? Are you persecuted? I don't mean are you in trouble because you're weird, strange, or a meddler and a busybody. The answer to that is you just need to control your tongue. But persecution is for the cross, the gospel. Paul says it will happen 'while evil men and impostors will go from bad to worse, deceiving and being deceived. But as for you, continue in what you have learned and what you have become convinced of' (vv.13–14).

I believe that when the Lord Jesus comes we're going to have revival unlike anything that we have seen in the history of the Church. It will make Pentecost seem like a raindrop! So people ask, 'Will the world get better and better, or will it get worse and worse?' The world will get simultaneously worse and worse and better and better, because God is going to restore the Church to power. It could happen any day, and it will be like the book of Acts, and the Church will have power unlike anything we have seen in centuries. But don't expect it to be better and better outside, because terrorism is increasing and we're also going to see persecution unlike anything previously.

Are you ready for it? Continue in the things that you have learned and have become convinced of. Realise that Scripture is of vital importance because it is 'God-breathed and is useful for teaching, rebuking, correcting and training in righteousness, so that the man of God may be thoroughly equipped for every good work' (vv.16–17). Some people are made by the times – treacherous, rash, conceited, lovers of pleasure, disobedient to parents, lovers of money, proud. Others are made for the times – 'As for you, continue in what you have learned and have become convinced of.' What about you?

ENDURANCE IN THE FACE OF OPPOSITION

ANDREW SAMPSON ON 2 TIMOTHY 3

The message of chapter 3 is introduced with a trumpet blast designed to alert Timothy to the truth about the seriousness of the times. 'Mark this,' Paul writes solemnly, 'there will be terrible times in the last days' (v.1). If we are to understand how these verses relate to our lives today a great deal depends on how we interpret the meaning of the 'last days'. The phrase is a frequent one in the Old Testament where it refers in a very general sense to 'the future', its precise meaning in any particular instance depending on the immediate context in which it is placed.[1] In the New Testament, however, the 'last days' are understood as referring specifically to the final phase of salvation history, inaugurated by the first coming of Christ (Heb. 1:2) and characterised by the presence of the Spirit (Acts 2:17). These are the days in which we now live, and hence it is relatively straightforward to make a connection between Timothy's circumstances and our own. In this chapter my concern is to show that if we are to take our discipleship seriously, we too need to heed Paul's warning and treat it with the seriousness it deserves.

In our increasingly complex world there are large numbers of things that justifiably warrant our concern. In the United Kingdom we find ourselves being perpetually thrown from one 'crisis' to another, whether centred on the threat posed by terrorism, unemployment, asylum seekers, pensions, education, unruly youth, global warming or the latest health scare. We are familiar with, and indeed accepting of, those social commentators who pronounce in doleful tones, and with varying degrees of accuracy, the measures we should be taking to prepare ourselves for the worst. In 2 Timothy 3:1, however, the terror Paul refers to is not the danger of social disintegration or of natural disaster, but the subtle, twisted inclinations of people's hearts and the degraded practices that result from them. What follows is a catalogue of 19 vices (vv.2–5), the very incoherence of which 'leaves the powerful impression of moral anarchy'.[2] But while Paul makes little obvious effort to group these evils in a particular way, it is interesting to note the manner in which he starts his list. John Calvin is not the only commentator to note that '*self-love*, which is put first, may be regarded as the source from which flow all the vices that follow afterwards'.[3] What Paul calls self-love is the essence of what he elsewhere terms 'sin', the fallen condition of humankind that causes us to put our own desires over and above our responsibilities to others and, especially, to God. It is the universal curse that has terrorised the human race throughout the ages, and to which men and women are still held captive today.

Three consequences tend to follow when people's love is directed in on themselves. The first is that they place a premium on 'feeling good'. Hence people become 'lovers of money' and pleasure (vv.2,4), their lives marked by a chronic lack of self-control as they seek to indulge their insatiable appetites for more (v.3). The second consequence is that people's relationships with one another begin to flounder and disintegrate. They become 'boastful', 'proud' and, even worse, 'brutal', 'treacherous', 'abusive', 'ungrateful', 'unforgiving' and 'slanderous' towards one another (vv.2–4). But the third consequence is in some ways the most disturbing of all: people become entrapped in the grip of false teaching that leads them to deny the true gospel and put their hope in any number of alternative, speculative ideologies. We make a great mistake if we suppose that those who are 'lovers of themselves' will turn their backs on religion altogether. Paul tells Timothy he can expect to meet many who make a show of the fact they are 'religious' but who demonstrate by their words and actions that they lack the inner reality of a changed heart (v.5). A religiosity that depends wholly on rite and ritual may offer a degree of comfort to the communicant, but without the power to remove the stain of sin from the human heart it is entirely devoid of substance in the eyes of God. The outer shell of a human life may look attractive on the outside but it is testimony to the power of the gospel only when there is a new creature inside (2 Cor. 5:17).

In fact, when reading this passage as a whole it quickly becomes clear that Paul reserves his harshest criticism not for those 'sinners' whose lifestyles fail to meet the moral requirements of the law of God, but for the 'religious people' who, having rejected his teaching, now try to persuade others to accept an alternative ideology in its place. It is these people who most exemplify the potential of selfish hearts to threaten the ministry of the gospel. Paul, therefore, does not mince his words in describing them as evil imposters (v.13) and 'men of depraved minds' whose lives are given over to folly (vv.8–9).

Timothy, however, is to be quite different. On two occasions Paul draws a clear contrast between the nature of his young protégé and that of the false teachers who fill Ephesus with their deception: 'You, however …' (v.10); 'But as for you …' (v.14).

Timothy differs fundamentally from the false teachers in one crucial respect: he is not given over to the dangerous narcissism of self-love but to the liberating experience of loving God. As a consequence everything about him is utterly different; he is truly distinctive. And the central message of chapter 3 is exactly this: we, too, are to be distinctive from those who ride the currents of self-interest.

Over the years many Christians have completely mis-understood the nature of our calling to distinctiveness. There is a peculiar brand of narrow-minded evangelicalism that sees the world as intrinsically evil and to be avoided at all costs. Even though most of us would not go that far, we may limit our involvement with the world as far as possible in order to avoid the risk of contamination with ungodly values and influences. Many of us look forward to our weekly retreats to the comfortable confines of Christian meetings, because it is only when we are with like-minded brothers and sisters that we feel we can truly 'be ourselves'. It is as we acknowledge and celebrate our faith in the context of Christian fellowship that the sharp distinction between our beliefs and the beliefs of the world truly comes to light.

Needless to say, authentic Christianity knows nothing of this kind of distinctiveness. For Jesus, the distinctiveness of His disciples from the world did not mean their physical separation from it but their moral dissociation from it. In John 17 He prays to His Father, 'As you sent me into the world, I have sent them [my disciples] into the world' (v.18). God loves the world, and we are therefore not to withdraw from it but to see it as the object of His love and the beneficiary of His saving grace (cf. John 3:16). In the same prayer, however, Jesus declares that His disciples 'are not of the world, even as I am not of it' (v.16). This world, although good, has been corrupted by the stain of wickedness and therefore cannot constitute the final dwelling place for those whom Christ has redeemed from the curse of sin. Our homeland is elsewhere, and hence the values by which we live our lives are quite literally 'other-worldly'.

We are called to be in the world but not of it. This kind of existence is extremely difficult to maintain because there are two alternatives infinitely more attractive in terms of the comfort they offer. It is much easier for us to hide ourselves away in our Christian cliques and live out our days in the context of the encouragement we find there. On the other hand, it is easy for us to give up on our distinctiveness altogether and to become indistinguishable from those who live according to the values of the world. What is difficult for us is to live in contact with the world while standing out from it as people who are 'different'. It is difficult precisely because there will come times when to stand up for the cause of Christ means we have to refuse to comply with the practices of those whose love is turned in on themselves, thereby risking their rejection and antagonism. To be in the world but not of it means that we will suffer.

Sharing in His suffering

The second letter to the Corinthians is, alongside this book, the most intensely personal of all Paul's epistles. In 2 Corinthians, Paul builds an argument to show how his ministry is fundamentally different from that of the self-appointed, apostolic pretenders who were touring the churches at that time. The letter is remarkable for its wealth of references to the theme of suffering, for this is the point at which Paul's own theological understanding differs most radically from that of his opponents. For Paul, suffering is a badge of honour that identifies him as belonging to his Saviour, showing him to be a true purveyor of the gospel of Christ (2 Cor. 6:4–10).

Hence Paul brings up the subject of his sufferings time and time again in order to commend his message and his ministry to the Corinthians.

We find Paul doing exactly the same thing in 2 Timothy 3 where, in verse 11, he points to his experience of suffering as authenticating his ministry. Timothy evidently needs little reminding of what Paul has been through ('You, however, know ...') for he has seen with his own eyes the suffering that distinguishes the ministry of his mentor from that of the false teachers. Then Paul goes on to say something breathtakingly bold. Starting from his personal experience he extrapolates to arrive at a universal rule that characterises the life of every Christian believer. 'In fact,' he writes, 'everyone who wants to live a godly life in Christ Jesus will be persecuted' (v.12). What a statement! He says 'everyone', and that means you and me. It is the inescapable consequence of living a life of distinctiveness in a world tainted by sin.

The New Testament writers make it clear that there is a type of suffering that belongs specifically to the Christian. It is true that we suffer by virtue of the fact that, along with the rest of humanity, we inhabit frail bodies that are subject to frustration and decay, but there is a second type of suffering, on top of that, which is peculiar to us alone. It is the suffering that results from our rejection by the world because of our identification with Christ.

Jesus Himself makes it clear to His disciples that the road of authentic discipleship is marked by the sign of the cross, the ultimate symbol of suffering: 'If anyone would come after me, he must ... take up his cross and follow me' (Matt. 10:38; Mark 8:34; Luke 9:23; 14:27). This theme is taken up in the great classic *The Cost of Discipleship* by Dietrich Bonhoeffer, a German pastor–theologian who lived in the first half of the twentieth century. In Chapter Four of his book Bonhoeffer includes a commentary on Jesus' familiar words:

> To endure the cross is not a tragedy; it is the suffering which is the fruit of an exclusive allegiance to Jesus Christ. When it comes it is not an accident, but a necessity. It is not the sort of suffering which is inseparable from this mortal life, but the suffering which is an essential part of the specifically Christian life. It is not suffering *per se* but suffering-and-rejection, and not rejection for any cause or conviction of our own, but rejection for the sake of Christ. ... The cross means sharing the suffering of Christ to the last and to the fullest.[4]

Bonhoeffer not only wrote these words; he lived them. Born in 1906 in Breslau, Germany, Bonhoeffer's family encouraged him to pursue his strong interest in theology from the age of 14. He was a young lecturer in systematic theology at Berlin University when Hitler came to power in 1933. Bonhoeffer rapidly became uneasy with his university's apparent indifference towards Hitler and he left his position in order to become a spokesman for the Confessing Church of Germany. As National Socialism increased its grip on his beloved nation, Bonhoeffer gave himself to trying to raise awareness of the threat that Socialist ideology posed to biblical Christianity. It was in this context that *The Cost of Discipleship* was first published, in 1937.

Two years later Bonhoeffer received an invitation to conduct pastoral work and theological training among German refugees in the United States. Bonhoeffer set sail for New York in June 1939 but quickly realised he had made the wrong decision.

He could not bear to be parted from his homeland at such a critical time in its history so he immediately turned around and returned to Germany. This was Bonhoeffer's moment of truth. It was a decision against the promise of security and for the cause of Christ with no regard for the consequences that might follow. Back in his homeland Bonhoeffer's name became synonymous with the underground resistance movement so that, in September 1940, he was forbidden to publish or speak in public and ordered to keep the police informed of his whereabouts. In April 1943 Bonhoeffer was arrested and imprisoned without trial. One of the last messages received from him while he was in prison was a poem entitled 'New Year 1945', the third verse of which reads:

> Should it be ours to drain the cup of grieving
> even to the dregs of pain, at thy command,
> we will not falter, thankfully receiving
> all that is given by thy loving hand.[5]

Dietrich Bonhoeffer was executed at Flossenburg concentration camp on 9 April 1945, several days before its liberation by the Allied forces.

We may not all be called to lay down our lives for the cause of Christ but we all are called to be prepared to do so. Biblically speaking, authentic Christian discipleship means being identified with Jesus Christ, and this necessarily entails the readiness to experience in our own lives the hostility that was directed towards and endured by our Saviour. It is the readiness to participate in what Lesslie Newbigin calls 'the messianic tribulation', 'the suffering which occurs at that point where the reign of God in Jesus challenges the powers of evil ranged against it'.[6] In the same way as Jesus stood up for the truth and received opposition from those whose hearts were turned against God, so we should expect to receive the same by virtue of our identification with Him.

Paul is very clear on this. He regards his identification with Christ as so close, so intimate, that the sufferings he endures in his body are in some sense an extension of the very same sufferings that Christ endured in His own. Paul can therefore write to the Corinthian church, 'The sufferings of Christ flow over into our lives' (2 Cor. 1:5), and 'We always carry around in our body the death of Jesus' (2 Cor. 4:10). To the Galatians he writes, 'I bear on my body the marks of Jesus' (Gal. 6:17) and, most astonishingly of all, he tells the Colossians, 'I fill up in my flesh what is still lacking in regard to Christ's afflictions' (Col. 1:24). For Paul this is not merely the lot of being an apostle, he expects it to be the experience of every disciple of Christ Jesus (cf. Phil. 1:29–30). In fact, our future inheritance of glory is itself dependent on us sharing in His sufferings (Rom. 8:17).

For most of us in the Western world today this aspect of Christian discipleship is largely absent from our lives. There is an extent to which the freedoms we enjoy in our culture offer us protection against the hostility of those who reject Christ and the truth He stands for. The world of Paul and his contemporaries is so far removed from our own that we barely notice the centrality of suffering to the New Testament's view of discipleship. When it does occasionally come to the surface through preaching or worship, the call of the disciple to share in the suffering of Christ is so alien to our established way of thinking, so incongruous to our theological frame of reference, that it often fails to register in our hearts and minds.

For example, in his famous song *All I once held dear*, Graham

Kendrick incorporates Paul's statement from Philippians 3 that our future hope is conditional on us sharing in the sufferings of Christ in the here and now (vv.10–11):

> Oh, to know the pow'r of Your risen life,
> and to know You in Your sufferings.
> To become like You in Your death, my Lord,
> so with You to live and never die.[7]

What do these words mean? They are a restatement of Paul's great ambition to be found in Christ and to lay aside everything that does not find its centre in his Saviour. For Paul this meant abandoning everything he previously considered to be of supreme value: his Jewish upbringing, his zeal for the law, his impressive moral stature, even his comfort and security. Paul reminds the Philippians that Jesus rejected the easy road of using His divine nature to His advantage, choosing instead to walk in obedience to the will of the Father on the road marked by rejection, opposition and, eventually, death (Phil. 2:6–8). In the same way, those who belong to Christ are called to make themselves 'nothing' and embrace the will of the Father in an attitude of humble obedience, no matter where it may take them. When we sing these words together we are declaring the truth that we, too, are called to identify with Christ in the manner of His suffering, for it is only by becoming one with Him in the shame of His death that we can be assured of being one with Him in the glory of His resurrection.

Yet so many of us want the glory without the shame, the resurrection without the dying. Kendrick's words are sung with great enthusiasm in our churches, but how many of us to stop to consider what they mean? Do we appreciate the gravity of what it means to share the great ambition of the apostle? Do we expect to experience the pain of opposition and persecution in our lives, or do we seek to avoid it altogether by removing ourselves from situations where our stand for the truth will be challenged?

Paul says, 'Everyone who wants to live a godly life in Christ Jesus will persecuted' (v.12), yet for Christians in the Western world persecution when it occurs is largely an oddity and an anomaly. It is, of course, altogether different for many of our brothers and sisters in the non-Western world for whom sharing in Christ's sufferings is a very real possibility and a daily experience. In our own nation large numbers of our young people also understand this, although admittedly to a less marked degree. A few years ago, when I was employed as a church youth worker, members of my youth group would come to me regularly and relate stories about the opposition they were experiencing in their schools as a direct consequence of standing up for the cause of Christ. One day, when I sat down with the group and asked them which themes they would like our Bible study series to address, the question that topped the list was, 'Why do people laugh at me when I say I am a Christian?'

It is very probable that this kind of opposition will increasingly become part of our common experience in the years to come. In a post 9/11 world struggling to come to terms with the new threat of global terrorism, people are becoming distrustful of those who adhere to any kind of organised religion that encourages activism in its members. We live in a society that esteems tolerance as the highest value so that, somewhat paradoxically, the opportunities for members of religious groups to express their stance on contentious issues are drastically curbed. Any religious system with a dogmatic claim to exclusivity is seen as narrow, discriminatory or downright dangerous. As a result it will become increasingly difficult for Christians in our culture to declare Jesus as the 'only way' without courting the hostility of the world. This is the conviction of Rob Frost who serves as the president of Release International, a charity that works to raise awareness of and support for persecuted Christians around the world. In his 2004 inaugural presidential address Frost issued the following warning:

> We are closer to persecution today than at any time in my life … Persecution is imminent. The message has to go out to young emerging leaders in the UK that Christianity is worth suffering for, and even dying for. It is not a game but a high-risk occupation.[8]

Stay the course

Paul is keenly aware of the risks posed to Timothy as a minister of the gospel in Ephesus. There can be no doubt that Timothy will at times be tempted to give in to pressure and relinquish his call to stand up for Christ. As a consequence Paul writes to persuade him to stay the course: 'As for you, continue in what you have learned and have become convinced of' (v.14a).

Before the sophisticated satellite-based navigation systems we use today ships used to be dependent on beacons to prevent them from straying off course. In my home county of Cornwall the coastline was at one time marked by a multitude of carefully placed beacons, each one designed to alert a ship to the danger of straying into the unforgiving rocks that lay nearby. In the event of a ship finding itself in jeopardy, the comforting sight of a light splicing the darkness would be the means by which the ship could check its course and point itself in the right direction. In this letter, Paul cites two things that will give Timothy the guidance to steer by, two beacons by which he can navigate successfully the chaotic waters of the times and persevere with the course set before him.

First, Timothy has the light of Paul's example to inspire and remind him that the Lord always comes to the rescue of those who are His (vv.14b, 11b). Here we find a clear example of Paul's strategy of commending himself as a model to be followed (see chapter 1). But there is something else designed to motivate and embolden Timothy to stay the course. In a previous age, there were men and women who used to line the cliffs of Cornwall when they spied a cargo vessel making its way around the coastline. The Cornish 'wreckers', as they were called, would hold up lanterns with the deliberate intention of confusing the ship's course and luring it on to the sharp rocks below. With the ship's fate sealed the wreckers would make their way to the base of the cliff, awaiting the vessel's demise and their opportunity to plunder its cargo. For any ship finding itself in troubled waters around Cornwall, it was therefore necessary not merely to have the aid of a light, but to have the aid of a light that could be trusted not to deceive.

For Timothy it is to be the Scriptures he has known from infancy that are to illuminate his path (v.15; cf. Psa. 119:105). The Scriptures will not only keep Timothy on course, but, in showing up every other pale fleck of luminosity that arises on the horizon for what it is, they will enable him to steer clear of those allurements that might otherwise ground him on the rocks. It is the Scriptures alone that make us 'wise for salvation through faith in Christ Jesus', and in saying this Paul is almost certainly alerting Timothy to how they contrast with the 'folly' offered by the false teachers (v.9b).

Paul highlights two characteristics of the Scriptures that

necessitate them being given prime importance in the Christian life. First, Paul points to their *authority*: 'All Scripture is God-breathed' (v.16a). Although it was men who wrote the words on the page, the prime authorship belongs to God as He carried along His prophets 'by the Holy Spirit' (2 Pet. 1:21). The Bible is therefore in an entirely different category to any other work of literature. It is not to be regarded merely as a 'good read' but as the Word of God which, in showing us what is eternally true, sets out the standard by which every other truth claim is to be judged. John Eldredge notes that our world 'is a carnival of counterfeits'.[9] How else, apart from the Word, are we to distinguish between the truth and the falsehood which subtly and insidiously commends itself to us as truth? Only the Word can keep us on course.

Second, Paul points to the Scriptures' *sufficiency*: 'So that the man of God may be thoroughly equipped for every good work' (v.17). No further revelation is required. History holds no secret and the human mind can conceive of no idea that can add one jot to what Scripture teaches about knowing the purposes of God for our lives. The Bible is the only tool we need for 'teaching, rebuking, correcting and training in righteousness' (v.16b) because it stands alone in telling us the story of salvation-history that is centred in, and leads us to, the Person and work of Jesus Christ. This is not to say that we cannot glean insights from additional sources, but these texts can help us in our pursuit of godliness only to the extent that they expound and apply biblical truth in accordance with biblical norms. With God's Word in hand we are fully equipped to continue our course, guard against error and bring guidance to those other ships we find struggling to negotiate the stormy waters.

Conclusion

In this chapter my concern has been to show how Paul's warning to Timothy in verse 1 applies to our lives today. We, too, are to take note of the fact that 'there will be terrible times in the last days', seasons when we will experience the hostility of those whose hearts are turned away from God. The extent to which we will suffer depends on the extent to which we are prepared to live distinctive, godly lives in the world. But lest our hearts are tempted to grieve, let us remember it is our privilege to identify with our Saviour in sharing His suffering. To those who count their suffering as joy (James 1:2) is given the promise not only of future glory (Matt. 5:12; Phil. 3:11) but a deeper, richer communion with Jesus in the here and now (Phil. 3:10). As Bonhoeffer writes:

> To go one's way under the sign of the cross is not misery and desperation, but peace and refreshment for the soul, it is the highest joy … Under his yoke we are certain of his nearness and communion. It is he whom the disciple finds as he lifts up his cross.[10]

Throughout history some of the greatest saints have been reformed and transformed through experiencing the nearness of Christ in the place of persecution. It is when we draw near to Him in the midst of His suffering that He draws near to us. Perhaps the reason many of us do not experience Him much is because we are not prepared to suffer much.

CHAPTER FOUR

2 TIMOTHY 4

PREACH THE WORD
R.T. KENDALL

OUR ETERNAL HOME
ANDREW SAMPSON

2 TIMOTHY 4

[1] In the presence of God and of Christ Jesus, who will judge the living and the dead, and in view of his appearing and his kingdom, I give you this charge:

[2] Preach the Word; be prepared in season and out of season; correct, rebuke and encourage – with great patience and careful instruction.

[3] For the time will come when men will not put up with sound doctrine. Instead, to suit their own desires, they will gather around them a great number of teachers to say what their itching ears want to hear.

[4] They will turn their ears away from the truth and turn aside to myths.

[5] But you, keep your head in all situations, endure hardship, do the work of an evangelist, discharge all the duties of your ministry.

[6] For I am already being poured out like a drink offering, and the time has come for my departure.

[7] I have fought the good fight, I have finished the race, I have kept the faith.

[8] Now there is in store for me the crown of righteousness, which the Lord, the righteous Judge, will award to me on that day – and not only to me, but also to all who have longed for his appearing.

Personal Remarks

⁹ Do your best to come to me quickly,

¹⁰ for Demas, because he loved this world, has deserted me and has gone to Thessalonica. Crescens has gone to Galatia, and Titus to Dalmatia.

¹¹ Only Luke is with me. Get Mark and bring him with you, because he is helpful to me in my ministry.

¹² I sent Tychicus to Ephesus.

¹³ When you come, bring the cloak that I left with Carpus at Troas, and my scrolls, especially the parchments.

¹⁴ Alexander the metalworker did me a great deal of harm. The Lord will repay him for what he has done.

¹⁵ You too should be on your guard against him, because he strongly opposed our message.

¹⁶ At my first defence, no-one came to my support, but everyone deserted me. May it not be held against them.

¹⁷ But the Lord stood at my side and gave me strength, so that through me the message might be fully proclaimed and all the Gentiles might hear it. And I was delivered from the lion's mouth.

¹⁸ The Lord will rescue me from every evil attack and will bring me safely to his heavenly kingdom. To him be glory for ever and ever. Amen.

Final Greetings

¹⁹ Greet Priscilla and Aquila and the household of Onesiphorus.

²⁰ Erastus stayed in Corinth, and I left Trophimus sick in Miletus.

²¹ Do your best to get here before winter. Eubulus greets you, and so do Pudens, Linus, Claudia and all the brothers.

²² The Lord be with your spirit. Grace be with you.

PREACH THE WORD!

R.T. KENDALL ON 2 TIMOTHY 4

Uppermost in some people's minds when facing death is how they will be remembered. But not Paul – all he cared about was the gospel. This man wrote almost two-thirds of the New Testament, gave Christianity its shape and did more to spread it than all the other apostles combined. It's hard to label him with one word. He was a theologian, teacher, evangelist, missionary, pastor and mentor. So we're going to look at what mattered most to him.

We saw at the end of chapter 3 the witness of revelation: 'All Scripture is God-breathed' (v.16). Peter echoes this: 'No prophecy of Scripture came about by the prophet's own interpretation. For prophecy never had its origin in the will of man, but men spoke from God as they were carried along by the Holy Spirit' (2 Pet. 1:20–21). The greatest product of the Holy Spirit is the Bible. The third Person of the Trinity is the author of Scripture – *all* Scripture. It's not a question of picking and choosing what you think is really from God and what you think isn't. Jesus confirms the origin of Scripture in Matthew 22:43 by quoting a reference to Himself in the Old Testament: '... David, speaking by the Spirit, calls him "Lord" ... '. Acts 4:25 echoes this: 'You spoke by the Holy Spirit through the mouth of your servant ... David.'

Whenever a church, or a minister, begins to question the infallibility of the Word of God, something inevitably goes wrong and that ministry, church or denomination will never be the same again. The best way to know the Bible as the Word of God is to be on good terms with the One who wrote it. The Holy Spirit is likened in the New Testament to a dove, a very sensitive bird. After John the Baptist had baptised Jesus, the Spirit of God descended 'like a dove' and alighted on Him, confirming to John that Jesus was the Son of God (Matt. 3:16). A dove usually comes down and immediately flies away, but He stayed on Jesus. And often when the Spirit comes down and we feel His presence we don't want Him to leave. But He can quickly fly away because He's so sensitive and can easily be grieved by what we do.

Normally such hypersensitivity is associated with the negative – an uncomplimentary reference to someone whose feelings are too easily hurt. But the Holy Spirit is hypersensitive in the right sense – and we need to understand this. The chief ways of grieving Him are bitterness, anger and being unforgiving. If you want to ensure that the dove will come down and stay, make sure you have totally forgiven everyone who has hurt you in any way. Then the Spirit will come and will make the Bible come alive. When someone begins to question Scripture it can often be traced back to bitterness and anger, which prevents them from being able to discern that it is God who is speaking.

Reinforcing his statement that all Scripture is 'God-breathed', Paul points to its authority: 'All Scripture ... is useful for teaching, rebuking, correcting and training in righteousness.' Scripture must be applied. We have no choice in what to teach or preach. Paul probably had one of the highest IQs in the history of mankind and if anybody had the genius to be creative, it was he. His genius was that he never tried to improve on the Word of God, never thought of saying anything new. He passed on the pure gospel. If you want to be a fool, try to upstage Scripture.

That's what happened in the Early Church. The Gnostics came along and said, in effect, 'Now look, your Christianity is wonderful, great, but we can make it even better.' But all they did was distort it – the greatest threat to the Church at that time. A modern equivalent is the New Age movement. The offer of something better through adding to Scripture is a lie of the devil.

'Preach the Word' (v.2)

Now, at the beginning of chapter 4, Paul turns to the challenge of always being ready to share the Word of God: 'In the presence of God and of Christ Jesus, who will judge the living and the dead, and in view of his appearing and his kingdom, I give you this charge: Preach the Word ...' (vv.1–2). It's very interesting that the apostle gives an eschatological introduction to this section – Jesus is actually coming back. It's a throwaway line, but Jesus' second coming is so real that Paul didn't feel the need to make a big issue of it. He just wanted to remind Timothy that Jesus is coming back again.

I will never forget a young man who was converted through a tract that we'd written at Westminster Chapel. He found it on High Street, Kensington, read it and was converted to Christ. About four months later he came up to me after a service and asked, 'Did I hear something about Jesus coming back?' I said 'Yes.' He said, 'You're saying that Jesus who came and died is coming back again?' I said 'Yes.' He said, 'That's wonderful, isn't it?' I said, 'Yes.' It just hit him that way. Jesus is coming again. In fact, says Paul, there is reward for all who long for His return (v.8).

Jesus is not only coming back, but His return will be as 'the righteous Judge,' says the apostle (v.8). Acts 17:31 says God the

Father 'has set a day when he will judge the world ... by the man he has appointed'. Paul here tells us who Jesus will judge – 'the living and the dead'. We're all going to be there! 'I saw a great white throne,' said the apostle John in Revelation, 'and him who was seated on it. Earth and sky fled from his presence ... The sea gave up the dead that were in it ...' (Rev. 20:11,13). It doesn't matter if a person is buried, cremated or drowned at sea: the God who made everyone will bring us all back. Converted or unconverted, living or dead, each of us will be summoned to stand before God to be judged.

Paul's comment about the second coming is followed by an essential instruction: 'Preach the Word'. Preach it, he says, 'in season and out of season.' What does he mean by this? Preaching it 'in season' is when you feel like it; preaching it 'out of season' is when you don't feel like it.

I used to sing an old spiritual: 'Every time I feel the Spirit moving in my heart, I'll pray.' Who wouldn't? The problem is that if I waited until I felt the Spirit moving in my heart, I'm not sure I would pray much at all! I don't often feel led to pray – I just do it. I don't feel like it – I just do it. If you want to be a mature Christian don't wait until you feel like praying: just do it. It's the same with preaching; there'll be times when, if you are a minister, pastor, church leader or lay preacher, you don't want to go into the pulpit. You'll think, 'I can't face them today.' Do it anyway – in season, out of season. Preach when God hides His face. But do it in an encouraging way. He doesn't want you to become one who lapses into moralising all the time – always pointing the finger. Preaching like that doesn't encourage. You do need to rebuke, but you also need to encourage, as Paul says, 'with great patience and careful instruction' (v.2).

Then Paul says, sadly, that there will be an angry reaction.

'For the time will come when men will not put up with sound doctrine' (v.3). That's a prediction. During an 'in season', you think, 'This is wonderful!' When God comes in great power you think nothing is ever going to change. But all revivals and times of great blessing come to an end. I wish it weren't so, but it is. It's like Peter on the Mount of Transfiguration: 'Lord, let's stay right here!' he said in effect (Matt. 17:4). But we have to come down from the mountain.

Revivals do end. The Lord does hide His face. And the time will come when people will not put up with the pure Word of God – 'sound doctrine'. Instead, says Paul, they will find 'a great number of teachers to say what their itching ears want to hear'. What they want to hear are things that suit their own desires and keep them in their comfort zones, rather than be stirred by the prophetic Word and challenged by powerful preaching that will make them change their lives.

There was a man in America some years ago who wasn't much of a preacher, but a church called him to minister. He had only one sermon and he preached it for a whole year. At the end of that year he had to face a review and told his wife that he didn't think he would be asked to continue. But he was given a unanimous vote to stay. Pleased, he tried his best to preach better but he still had basically only one sermon. So at the end of the second year he and his wife began to pack. But he got a unanimous vote again. He was thrilled and tried and tried to improve in the third year, but he just couldn't do it. He was desperately hunting for another job but, lo and behold, yet another unanimous vote came for him to stay on. So he said to the chief deacon, 'Look, you know and I know I can't preach. Yet you keep giving me a unanimous vote to stay. Why?' 'Oh,' said the deacon, 'the answer is very simple. We never wanted a preacher in the first place!' The congregation was happy with somebody who would not stir them. There are many churches like that.

An evangelist called Rolfe Barnard was visiting a church in Oklahoma, USA, and the pastor, knowing his reputation for sometimes coming in with John the Baptist-like challenges, said: 'Now folks, we all want revival but we don't want a stir.' Revival never comes in a neat and tidy package.

Paul tells Timothy: 'Endure hardship, do the work of an evangelist' (v.5). Never forget the gospel. Church leaders should be soul winners. This is what changed my life. It happened in 1982 when Arthur Blessitt came to Westminster Chapel, mightily challenged us about winning people to Christ and got us out on the streets telling people about Him. So I made a calculated decision that I'd spend the rest of my ministry being a personal soul winner. I thought I had done my duty when I preached from the pulpit, but it's easier to preach to thousands than to talk to one person. I used to want to be a theologian but God said, 'Sorry RT, you're called to be an evangelist.' My ministry changed, my anointing doubled and I never looked back. We must not want to see the Church grow by transfer growth – people leaving one church to join another. That's not the way. Methodism grew out of people being saved right, left and centre.

'I have finished the race' (v.7)

Then, almost abruptly, Paul changes the subject and says in verse 6, 'For I am already being poured out like a drink offering, and the time has come for my departure.' 'Poured out like a drink offering.' I'd have wanted to say to Paul, 'Tell me more.' He might have said, 'You don't need to know.' But maybe when we get to heaven we'll find out. But here is the secret to the apostle's anointing: the greater the suffering, the greater God's power working through him.

Paul tells us what is at hand – his departure. Then in verse 7 comes a wonderful little autobiography: 'I have fought the good fight, I have finished the race, I have kept the faith.' I look forward to being able to say this when my time comes to depart from this earth to be with Christ. Do you?

There was a time when Paul wasn't so sure. Several years previously he had written to the Corinthians:

> Do you not know that in a race all runners run, but only one gets the prize? Run in such a way as to get the prize. Everyone who competes in the games goes into strict training. They do it to get a crown that will not last; but we do it to get a crown that will last for ever. Therefore I do not run like a man running aimlessly; I do not fight like a man beating the air. No, I beat my body and make it my slave so that after I have preached to others, I myself will not be disqualified for the prize. (1 Cor. 9:24–26)

Paul did not fear being lost, but he did fear not receiving a reward. The Authorised Version translates 'disqualified for the prize' as 'be a castaway'. It comes from the Greek word *adokimos*, which means rejected. Paul couldn't think of anything worse than seeing his converts get a reward while he himself missed out because he had become yesterday's man over some foolish sin. He knew himself only too well and he knew that if God didn't help him he could fall.

Billy Graham once said to a friend of mine that his greatest fear was that God would take His hand off him. It's also my greatest fear, because without His hand on me I am capable of anything. That's why Paul wrote that he took tough measures to keep his body under control. But he has changed his tone by the time he comes to write his second letter to Timothy. In effect he says, 'It'll be OK now because I have kept the faith and finished the race.' Because he has done so 'there is in store for me the crown of righteousness, which the Lord, the righteous Judge, will award to me' (v.8). He knew he'd got it now. Until you reach that moment, understand that you are capable of a serious fall and it would bring disgrace on God's name. Paul never took it for granted, because he knew he was weak. But now he says, 'I have kept the faith.'

Not so with some. Paul writes, 'Demas … has deserted me … Crescens has gone to Galatia … Only Luke is with me … Alexander the metalworker did me a great deal of harm. The Lord will repay him for what he has done' (vv.9–10,14). Others had deserted him when he most needed their support, but, he says, 'May it not be held against them' (v.16).

Paul is taken up with what awaits him at his departure from his earthly life because the greatest thing, next to going to heaven, is to receive a reward at the judgment seat of Christ. It's so important to understand this. You may think you don't care about this, that all you want to do is get to heaven, but you will regret it when the time comes. Charles Wesley's hymn got it right: ' … till we cast our crowns before Him'. But what if you don't have a crown to cast before Him? How will you feel on that day?

A reward – inheritance, prize and crown are descriptions used interchangeably – was very important to Paul. The apostle wanted it, and on that day you will want it. I can imagine nothing greater than hearing from the lips of Jesus Himself, 'RT, well done!' I would rather hear that than anything else. And

Paul said, 'I've got it! It's coming!' Get your theology right at this point: all who are saved will go to heaven, but not all who go to heaven will receive a reward at the judgment seat of Christ. You think, 'Well, I'm no apostle Paul.' Neither am I. But he doesn't say it's just for apostles: '... but also to all who have longed for his appearing' (v.8). If you are longing for Jesus to come, if you can't wait to see Him, you're in pretty good shape spiritually. You qualify.

Finally, we come to the secret of Paul's anointing. It reminds me of Stephen, who imitated Jesus' attitude on the cross, when He said, 'Father, forgive them, for they do not know what they are doing' (Luke 23:34). As Stephen was dying he said, 'Lord, do not hold this sin against them' (Acts 7:60). And Paul's last words, when he's lonely, hurt by his friends and fellow workers and waiting to depart from earth, are 'May it not be held against them.' Pray for your enemies. Totally forgive them, and pray that God will let them off the hook, because He has let you off the hook.

OUR ETERNAL HOME

ANDREW SAMPSON ON 2 TIMOTHY 4

In chapter 4 we come not only to the conclusion of the second letter to Timothy but to the last surviving words from the pen of Paul. It is possible that they are the last he ever had the opportunity to write. As the aged apostle manages the handing over of his ministry from within the confines of his cell, he is no doubt reflecting on the imminent threat of execution that hangs ominously over him. But in spite of the bleakness of his future, Paul's primary concern is not with himself. Anyone in a similar position might be justifiably excused for giving expression to sorrow or self-pity, but for Paul the inner cries of his frail humanity are of no consequence. The ministry of the gospel is greater than any man, so Paul directs his gaze outwards to the life of the young man he is counting on to take up his ministry in Ephesus. 'Timothy,' he urges, 'I give you this charge: Preach the Word' (vv.1b–2a).

This is to be Timothy's number one priority. The hope for the city of Ephesus rests in just this, that the local church, as the sign and instrument of God's kingdom, is once again converted to the gospel through the fearless proclamation of the Word of God. So crucial does Paul consider his charge to Timothy that he adds that he should 'be prepared in season and out of season' (v.2). As a minister of the Word, Timothy is to regard himself as being 'on call' at any time, ensuring that he possesses a readiness and an eagerness to respond to situations with the truth as and when they arise. In practice, Paul's injunction to Timothy prohibits him from excusing himself from ministering the Word in a situation merely because the moment is deemed 'inconvenient'. Nor is Timothy permitted to turn his back on an opportunity for sharing the Word because he finds himself in the 'wrong mood', or because people seem indifferent to what he has to say or disinclined to respond. Timothy is encouraged to view the preaching of the Word as more important than any other consideration, and so, once again, we see that he is being called to instil in his own life and ministry the values that have directed the life and ministry of Paul. The commentator Thomas Oden, reflecting on the situation of the apostle as he writes these words, makes the following observation: 'There is no forty-hour week for attesting the truth. It is a work that is fitting for any hour, any day, not merely in the service of worship but in the marketplace and home, not merely in freedom but in chains, not merely in comfort and security but precisely while facing death.'[1]

Here, then, is a clear and specific application for all those who serve as teachers and preachers of the Word. The handling of the Word is not to be consigned to a few slots in the week; rather it is to be an aspect of our everyday lives. Smith Wigglesworth (1859–1947), the extraordinary preacher who earned the nickname 'the apostle of faith', used to say that he did not consider himself to be properly dressed unless he had his Bible with him. The Word was literally a part of his wardrobe. In this way, Wigglesworth nurtured the same habit of readiness that Paul here commends to Timothy and was able to bring transformation to the lives of many individuals in the most ordinary of places. But in Paul's imperative we, too, find a more general application for all Christians. All of us are to be always 'on standby'. We are not to compartmentalise our lives into 'ministry' and 'other' so that the communication of the Word is relegated to those few activities that are popularly thought of as 'sacred'. The effective transmission of the gospel into the world depends on us living our lives in a state of constant readiness to bring the Word of God, our most precious of treasures, into the open. The Word is not only for the Church but for the world, not only for the sanctuary but for the street corner, and wherever it is taken it is to be unleashed and allowed to do its work in the hearts of men and women. God does not recognise the compartments we introduce into our lives for He sees what we are in private just as He sees what we are in public. He knows the extent to which we allow the Word to shape our lives in the workplace and in the place of the worship. He sees our lives as one seamless, coherent whole, and He will judge them as such.

When we keep this point in mind we begin to find ourselves viewing our lives in an entirely new light. Paul knows that Timothy needs every motivation to enter into his ministerial duties without compromise, so he abandons his previous practice of gentle encouragement through reminiscence and personal appeal. None of this can adequately convey the sense of gravity that is in keeping with what is to follow. So, for a moment, we catch a glimpse of Paul's absolute confidence in wielding his God-given authority as he thunders: 'In the presence of God and of Christ Jesus, who will judge the living and the dead, and in view of his appearing and his kingdom, I give you this charge ...' (v.1). In addressing Timothy in this way, Paul's words have the effect of turning the mind of his protégé towards those things that – unavoidably for a man in the last, short stretch of his life – loom large for him. 2 Timothy chapter 4 is highly future oriented, with the apostle extending his excerpts of testimony to incorporate not only the painful memories of his past but also his eagerly awaited future. The parallel passages in verses 6–8 and 16–18 show Paul's supreme confidence as he prepares to leave the 'earthly tent' of his body (2 Cor. 5:1), and serve to encourage Timothy to remain faithful in ministry so that he might have the same confidence also.

The material in these chapters by R.T. Kendall and myself was first presented at the Easter People conference under the theme of 'Destiny'. As Christians, there are two distinct senses in which we can speak of our destiny. First, there is the destiny that relates to our lives as temporal, historical beings, the calling that consists of God's specific plans for our earthly lives. But there is a second, grander aspect to our 'destiny'. This relates not to our transient pilgrimage here on earth but to our journey's ultimate destination, the 'heavenly kingdom' that constitutes our eternal home (v.18). We must not suppose that these different definitions relate to two disparate lives that lack connection with one another. For Paul, the character of the heavenly existence he hopes for is intricately connected with, and indeed dependent on, all that he has given himself to in this life. Similarly, Paul views his earthly life as possessing coherence and meaning because, and only because, it has reference to its future goal. Paul understands and lives by the principle that it is only when we have our future destination in mind that we are able to live godly lives in the here and now.

In what follows, I will be exploring the inter-connectedness of the present and future dimensions of our lives with reference to Paul's four injunctions to Timothy in verse 5. Throughout this chapter Paul is keen for Timothy to perceive his life and ministry anew through gaining a greater awareness and understanding of his ultimate destination. Paul stands a few steps away from his goal and Timothy has very many miles ahead of him yet, but both men can find the courage and conviction they need for the way ahead by considering the future. Here I hope to show that we can be helped in the same way.

1. 'Keep your head in all situations'

The parable of the lost son in Luke 15 is one of the best known and best loved of all Jesus' parables. The story starts with a son going to his father and demanding his share of the inheritance. The father – somewhat reluctantly we might suppose – agrees to the request, only to watch his son leave the estate for a 'distant country' and squander all his wealth in 'wild living' (v.13b). All goes well for the son at first, but even a sizeable fortune cannot withstand the self-indulgence of a young man experimenting with his newly-found freedom, and before long the money runs out. When a 'severe famine' hits the land (v.14) the son's impoverished state goes from bad to worse, and he is forced to earn his living working for a pig farmer. To his horror, his fellow Jews avoid him as a person as unclean as the animals he feeds, and his hunger becomes so intense that the pig feed begins to look as appetising as the sumptuous food he used to eat in his father's house.

His father's house! Now that the distractions of his hedonistic lifestyle are stripped away and the son has nothing to do but reflect on the sorry events of his journey, he realises that it need not be this way. Jesus says, 'he came to his senses' (v.17a). The intoxicating effect of worldly pleasures loses its hold and the son's mind is free to revaluate his life's direction and goal. It is the moment when he awakes spiritually, as from a nightmare, and now he sees the opportunities and threats that come his way in their true colours. How could he have been so foolish as to miss it all before?

Most of us make forays into the 'distant country' of the prodigal from time to time. We desire to remain in intimate communion with our heavenly Father and refuse the allurements of worldly pleasures, but the moment a questionable possibility of making money opens up to us, or a circle of people we admire starts trying to persuade us, or a pretty girl walks into the room, we all too easily lose our resolve and our honourable intentions melt away. In short, we know what it means to 'lose our senses', or, to use Paul's language here, 'lose our heads'. In the face of temptation our sound, sober judgment begins to dissipate and our ability to maintain our moral composure begins to erode. Like Timothy, we need to be reminded continually to 'keep your head in all situations'.

The significance of this first injunction to Timothy is well illustrated by the example of Demas, one of Paul's fellow-workers (Col. 4:14; Philem. 24) who later forsook him (v.10). When we make our treasure the comforts of the world, our hearts will no longer find the source of their delight in the gospel of Christ (cf. Matt. 6:21), and this will be enough to discount us from finding our place in the purposes of God.

Jesus warns His listeners time and time again that they cannot presume to enter the kingdom of God without first counting the cost and discounting everything that this world considers to be of value. The kingdom of God is like a treasure in a field or a fine pearl which, when found, demands the surrender of every other thing that is possessed in order to obtain it (Matt. 13:44–46). The allurements of this world, while dazzling in their beauty and enticing in their attractiveness, must be measured alongside the value of that which is quite literally priceless. It is this ability to 'measure things up', to ascribe to them their true value, which is the characteristic of those who 'keep their heads'. To do so it is necessary to remember that the treasures for which we strive are not those earthly treasures that last only for a time, but those heavenly treasures that will be ours to enjoy for ever.

We do not belong to this world! We are pilgrims passing through, travellers making our way to a homeland that is elsewhere. Consequently, we are not to allow the things of this world to become so dear to us that we forget where our true home lies. One of the major characteristics of our time and culture is that many are locked into the 'perpetual present' in which little thought is given to the morrow. What matters is what can be won *now*, what can be experienced *now*, what can be consumed *now*. As Christians we can live in plenty or in want, with possessions or without them, but we cannot afford to allow our minds to become conformed to the worldly ideal of 'instant gratification'. As Malcolm Muggeridge writes:

> I strain my ears to hear it, like distant music; my eyes to see it, a very bright light very far away ... The only ultimate disaster that can befall us, I have come to realise, is to feel ourselves to be at home here on earth. As long as we are aliens we cannot forget our true homeland.[2]

The apostle Peter, aiming to highlight the incongruity between a 'worldly' life and a distinctly Christian life, declares that we are 'aliens and strangers in this world' (1 Pet. 2:11). Paul says to the Philippians that we do not set our minds on earthly things because 'our citizenship is in heaven' (Phil. 3:20). Just as Timothy is called to be clear headed, so we too are called to exercise sober judgment in accordance with kingdom values. Do not get wrapped up in the things of this world; keep a clear perspective, and remember where your true homeland lies.

2. 'Endure hardship'

We have seen that one of Paul's purposes in writing this letter to Timothy is to warn him that he can expect to receive opposition from those who turn away from sound doctrine to false teaching (vv.3–4). Timothy is not to incline his ministry away from those given over to false teaching by ignoring them altogether. Such a move would be irresponsible for someone wielding the authoritative Word of God; moreover, it would prove impossible in practice for someone exercising a public leadership ministry. No, Timothy is called to enter into the fray with boldness and confidence. Hardship is therefore assured, and Paul directs Timothy's attention to one further principle that will enable him to endure it.

For the whole of his ministry Paul has laboured under the conviction that the hardship of opposition and rejection is a constructive force in the Christian life. It is the means by which a believer is marked out as belonging to Christ and is enabled to come to an intimate knowledge of His fellowship. Moreover, just as Christ's exaltation to the right hand of the Father was dependent on His suffering ('*therefore* God exalted him', Phil. 2:9a), so our experience of sharing in that suffering becomes the means by which we can be assured of one day sharing in His glory. The biblical principle is this: our hardship in this life is our guarantee of rich blessings in the next. Hardship for the sake of Christ is the harbinger of glory.

Paul therefore wants to persuade Timothy not to look at the hardships themselves but at the promise that lies beyond them. He is to refocus his eyes so that the glorious future that awaits him is seen with perfect clarity and allowed to inform his perception of all that he endures in the present. Elsewhere Paul writes, 'I consider that our present sufferings are not worth comparing with the glory that will be revealed in us' (Rom. 8:18). If the weight of the hardship we go through now could be compared with the weight of glory promised us in the future, the scales would tip overwhelmingly in favour of our future inheritance. In fact, Paul suggests that the comparison is not worth bothering with in the first place. The riches of the kingdom of heaven are so enormous in magnitude that the irritations suffered in this life do not even register on the scale. They are quite literally negligible.

This makes it possible for us to find the strength to endure even the most hurtful of life's experiences. If we who belong to Christ have the hope of glory alive in our hearts, our eyes become focused not on the afflictions that result from our identification with our Saviour but on the infinitely greater riches promised us in the future. Paul writes to the Corinthians: 'For our light and momentary troubles are achieving for us an eternal glory that far outweighs them all. So we fix our eyes not on what is seen, but on what is unseen. For what is seen is temporary, but what is unseen is eternal' (2 Cor. 4:17–18). The great Methodist hymn writer, Charles Wesley, puts it like this:

> In hope of that immortal crown,
> I now the cross sustain,
> And gladly wander up and down,
> And smile at toil and pain.
> I suffer out my threescore years,
> Til my Deliverer come,
> And wipe away His servant's tears,
> and take His exile home.[3]

The people who love this world may laugh at us for a time, but what is that compared to an eternity in glory? They may afflict us for our commitment to the gospel, but that pales into insignificance alongside the riches that God offers us. What is the worst they could do to us? Death itself is the gateway to glory and has been emptied of its horror. For us, as for Timothy, having an eternal perspective will enable us to stand up under whatever hardship comes our way.

3. 'Do the work of an evangelist'

The third injunction given to Timothy discloses Paul's burning conviction that the persistence of the gospel and the expansion of its sphere of influence depend on the commitment of men and women to pass it on. People do not usually receive the message of salvation via an inner light in their hearts while they sit in isolation, nor do they apprehend the truth through the philosophical meanderings of their minds. God is able to turn hearts and minds towards Him in even the remotest of places, yet He chooses to use His servants as instruments of the good news. Paul's famous words in Romans 10 therefore hold true: '... how can they hear without someone preaching to them?' (v.14b).

Consequently, Timothy is to shy away from the mentality that would cause him to limit his duties to those of a pastor or teacher in the Church. He is to see the scope of his ministry in much broader terms than that. Like Paul before him, he is to view his ministry as participation in the mission of God which has as its goal not merely the edification of believers but the inclusion of outsiders in the kingdom of God. One of the dominant themes of Scripture is that where previously the people of God had considered their blessing to be a private possession, now, in Christ, a new era of salvation history has been inaugurated, the kingdom has come, and the blessings of salvation are offered to all, irrespective of background or status.

It is time for the 'others' to come in (cf. Matt. 22:1–10) and the Church is called to be the community that manifests the inclusiveness of the kingdom in all its technicolour diversity.

For this reason the Church is never static: it is continually reaching out to those who are outside the kingdom. But a local church will be unlikely to take its missionary responsibility sufficiently seriously unless its leaders are first showing, by example, that outreach is a priority in their own lives. In being called to evangelism, Timothy is being called to exemplify, in microcosm, the missionary thrust of the Church that declares, 'The kingdom has come!'

However, this takes into account only one aspect of what the kingdom is all about. The peculiar nature of the kingdom of God (when compared to any other 'kingdom' we may think of) is seen in the fact that it has both a present and a future dimension: it is both 'now' and 'not yet'. Jesus says, for example, that His ability to command the spiritual forces of darkness is a sign that 'the kingdom of God has come upon you' (Matt. 12:28) yet a few chapters later He speaks of a time in the future when people will see 'the Son of Man [Jesus' designation of Himself] coming in his kingdom' (Matt. 16:28). The tension between Jesus' 'now' and 'not yet' descriptions of the kingdom is both deliberate and necessary, for the kingdom of God can be properly understood only when it is viewed as the future rule and reign of God breaking into and transforming human experience in the present. The manifold blessings we experience now by virtue of the fact that we accept God's lordship in our lives are but a foretaste of the greater blessings we shall experience when, at the consummation of history, the kingdom arrives in fullness. The meaning of the kingdom can therefore be summarised in this way: in the present it is realised only in part; in the future it will be realised in full.

When we relate this to Paul's third injunction to Timothy in verse 5, we can see that the task of evangelism is informed both by the present and future dimensions of the kingdom. In fact, the latter is more relevant to a discussion of this chapter in which both of Paul's references to the kingdom regard it solely in terms of the future (vv.1b,18). By fixing his eyes on the hope of the 'heavenly kingdom' (v.18), Timothy will find he possesses two significant tools to aid him in his evangelism: first, he is given a central plank of the gospel message, and second, he is given a major incentive to get on and share it. When we look at these two tools in detail we can choose whether to consider them positively or negatively. On the negative side, much has been made historically of the doctrine that unbelievers are in danger of hell, and this has often become a prominent theme of the evangelist's message and a powerful inducement to reaching the lost. For a balanced discussion on the extent to which the doctrine of hell should motivate us in evangelism, the reader is referred to the Evangelical Alliance's helpful report on *The Nature of Hell* (pp.112–118). My own view is in broad agreement with the authors of this paper that, biblically, 'the proclamation of the gospel is an invitation to abundant life before it is a warning against eternal damnation (eg Matt. 11:28; John 3:16; John 6:35ff; John 10:10; Rom. 6:23).[4] For this reason I restrict myself to a discussion of the positive ways in which a consideration of the future kingdom affects the work of the evangelist.

One of the twentieth century's greatest contributors to the Church's understanding of its missionary task was Lesslie Newbigin (1909–1998), an extraordinary pastor–scholar who for much of his working life served as a missionary in India. On his retirement and return to England in 1974, Newbigin found himself being asked frequently the question, 'What was the greatest difficulty you faced in moving from India to England?' In response, writes Newbigin, 'I have always answered, "The disappearance of hope." Even in the squalid slums of Madras there was always the belief that things could be improved ... In England, by contrast, it is hard to find any such hope.'[5] Against this kind of background there is a magnificent opportunity for the gospel to shine all the more brightly. The promise of the future arrival of the kingdom of God, heralded by Christ's return, is a powerful message that strikes at the heart of the despair and hopelessness felt by so many in our society. We do not offer empty words of comfort, for the promise rests on something concrete – the community of God's elect who are being 'transformed into his likeness with ever-increasing glory' (2 Cor. 3:18) as a sign and pledge of the coming kingdom. When people choose to submit to God's rule their circumstances may or may not change, but they are assured of receiving the blessings of the kingdom when it arrives in fullness, and enjoying them for ever.

The future character of the kingdom must therefore be allowed to inform the message of the evangelist. Secondly, it must be allowed to inform the motivation of the evangelist. For many years, men and women were moved to spread the gospel because of the threat of hell. If we turn this on its head we end up with an equally powerful incentive to evangelism: the hope of heaven. If we truly love those who do not love Christ then we will want to do all that we can to ensure that they, too, come to the point where they accept the promise of a place in the heavenly kingdom. A firm appreciation of what lies ahead of us will necessarily result in a renewed passion for evangelism because we simply cannot help but share the good news of our glorious hope.

When Paul presents his charge to Timothy 'in view of his appearing and his kingdom' these words are not designed merely to inject an air of solemnity into the apostle's words. They are telling Timothy that, as an evangelist, he is to keep firmly in view the message of hope that lies at the heart of the gospel. To do so will make Timothy a better evangelist. The same is also true of us.

4. 'Discharge all the duties of your ministry'

The story is told of an elderly carpenter who, after many years of faithful service to his contractor, was ready to retire. His employer was sorry to hear of his intention and asked if the carpenter would build just one more house as a personal favour. The carpenter agreed to this request, but as time went by it became clear that his heart was not in his work. He ordered in cheap materials that lacked durability and rushed through the project in extra quick time. When the employer came to inspect the finished building he found a piece of poor workmanship that utterly failed to do justice to the capabilities of the carpenter. Then, reaching into his pocket, the contractor produced a key and handed it to the carpenter. 'This is the key to the house,' he said. 'It is my gift to you for so many years of faithful service.'

Whether or not we perceive it, we are all making decisions in this life that contribute to the shape of our future habitation. In 1 Corinthians 3 Paul pictures leaders in the Church as workmen who choose to build either with valuable materials (gold, silver and costly stones) or worthless materials (wood, hay and straw). On the day of judgment, writes Paul, the quality of each person's contribution to the life of the Church will become clear to all as it is tested by fire. 'If what he has built survives, he will receive his reward. If it is burned up, he will suffer loss' (vv.14–15a). This is not to say that the second type of worker will be in danger of losing his salvation altogether for Paul adds, 'he himself will be saved, but only as one escaping through the flames' (v.15b). On the day of judgment there will be those whose failure to fulfil their earthly responsibilities means they make it to the heavenly kingdom only by the skin of their teeth and they will be refused any reward.

But this warning is not only for those in positions of leadership. The Bible makes it clear that, on the day when Christ returns to 'judge the living and the dead' (v.1), we will all appear before His judgment seat, 'that each one may receive what is due to him for the things done while in the body, whether good or bad' (2 Cor. 5:10; cf. Rom. 14:10; Rev. 22:12). Jesus speaks of the importance of storing up for ourselves 'treasures in heaven' (Matt. 6:20; 19:21; Luke 6:23,35; 12:33) which will be rewarded to us when He returns in glory with the angels (Matt. 16:27). The inescapable conclusion is that Jesus will judge all of us on the basis of our works of service, and our experience of life in the heavenly kingdom will be affected as a result.

As Paul considers these things from within his Roman prison cell, he reverts back to his former reflective mood and casts his mind back over many long years of Christian service. As he does so, he is filled with a confidence that he has faithfully discharged all the duties of his ministry. 'I have fought the good fight,' he declares, 'I have finished the race, I have kept the faith' (v.7). He is able to say that through him the gospel has been 'fully proclaimed' and 'all the Gentiles' have heard it (v.17). He knows that he has not gone about his work half-heartedly, he has not sidestepped his responsibility, he has not cut corners. The building materials he has used have been worthy of the foundation on which he has built, which is Christ (1 Cor. 3:11), and as a result he is confident that his workmanship will stand up to the Lord's scrutiny on the Last Day. He looks forward to receiving his reward, 'the crown of righteousness' (v.8a) that 'will last for ever' (1 Cor. 9:25b), and as he writes these words under the shadow of the executioner's sword this now seems tantalisingly close (v.6b).

In sharing these personal reflections with Timothy, and in keeping with the general theme of this letter, Paul is bringing his young protégé further encouragement for the difficult road ahead. Timothy is being given an incentive to give himself wholly to the ministry of the gospel so that he, like Paul before him, can look forward to receiving a rich reward from his Saviour on the Last Day. As he keeps one eye on his present labour in the Lord's service he is to keep the other firmly on the fact of future judgment. This is how he can ensure that when his workmanship is brought before the judge of all the earth, it will be for him a time of great joy rather than sorrow and regret. It is only as Timothy counts himself among those who 'set their hearts' on Christ's return (v.8b, NEB), that he can share the confidence of his mentor in facing the judgment seat of Christ.

We, too, need to be mindful of the fact that one day we will be required to give an account of all that we have done. In the meantime, we would do well to remember that what the Lord requires of us is that we discharge all the duties of *our* ministry, not someone else's. When, after what I hope will be a long and productive life, I stand before the judgment seat of Christ, He will not turn to me and say, 'Andrew, why did you not become the student pastor of a church when you were 20 years old? Why did you not witness to Yasser Arafat while there was still the chance? Why did you not minister at Westminster Chapel for 25 years?' There is a very good answer to all those questions: I am not R.T. Kendall. Too many of us beat ourselves up because we spend so much time comparing our work for the Lord with the work entrusted to someone else. But God gives to each one of us specific responsibilities and expects us to be faithful only in that which we are called to do. Then we will be able to look Jesus in the eye on that final day and say with confidence, 'I did all that you required of me' and hear in response those words that will cause our hearts to rejoice for the whole of eternity: 'Well done, good and faithful servant!' (Matt. 25:21, 23).

Conclusion

Throughout the discussion of this chapter my focus has been on the ways in which a knowledge of our ultimate destination affects how we understand and implement our calling in the here and now. Our hope of the victorious Christ coming again to judge the world causes us to see every choice we make in a new light. Our promise of a heavenly home in which the blessings of the kingdom have arrived in fullness means that we can never truly 'fit in' here on earth. In the words of the great missiologist David Bosch:

> We live within the creative tension between the already and the not yet, forever moving closer to the orbit of the former. We Christians are an anachronism in the world: not anymore what we used to be, but not yet what we are destined to be. We are too early for heaven, yet too late for the world. We live on the borderline between the already and the not yet. We are a fragment of the world to come, God's colony in a human world, his experimental garden on earth.[6]

Paul knows that, at times, Timothy will be trampled on and, like a frail young plant, struggle to hold his face in the light of the sun. So, in verse 22, Paul pronounces a blessing on the life of his nervous apprentice: 'The Lord be with your spirit.' As he does so, one can almost hear his aside, 'I know He will be,' for in the apostle's experience there was never a time when the Lord did not come to his rescue and give him the strength to endure (v.17).

In that first blessing of verse 22 the word 'your' is singular; Paul is directing that blessing to Timothy alone. But in the blessing that follows, 'Grace be with you,' the 'you' in the original Greek is plural. Perhaps we find here an indication that Paul intended this letter, not only for the readership of Timothy in a specific context and time, but for all believers like him, in all contexts and at all times. This short statement is Paul's final bequest to the Church, and throughout the ages it has been the means by which his blessing has been pronounced on the life of every weary Christian that has sought comfort and strength from his words. It is a blessing on your life and mine, expressing the apostle's supreme confidence that God will give to each one of us the grace for what lies ahead.

NOTES

Chapter One

1. See Chapter 1 of *Pure Joy* by R.T. Kendall (Hodder & Stoughton, 2004) for a further explanation on God allowing suffering.

2. F.W. Boreham, *Dreams at Sunset* (London: Epworth Press, 1954) p.53.

3. J. Monod, *Chance and Necessity: An Essay on the Natural Philosophy of Modern Biology* (London: Collins, 1972) p.167.

4. See also the Westminster Catechism. 'Question 1: What is the chief and highest end of man? Answer: Man's chief and highest end is to glorify God, and fully to enjoy him for ever.'

5. This phrase, attributed to the word of the Lord when He halted Saul (Paul) the Pharisee on the road to Damascus, was a popular proverb in the first century. It was a way of expressing the struggle against one's destiny. See I.H. Marshall, *The Acts of the Apostles* (Leicester: Inter-Varsity Press & Grand Rapids: Eerdmans, 1980, reprinted 1999) p.395.

6. I heard this illustration used by Nicky Gumbel but I have been unable to track down the original source.

7. T.C. Oden, *First and Second Timothy and Titus* (Louisville: John Knox Press, 1989) p.31.

8. G.D. Fee, *God's Empowering Presence: The Holy Spirit in the Letters of Paul* (Peabody: Hendrickson, 1994) p.791.

9. See Gordon Fee's excellent book of this title.

10. L. Newbigin, *A Word in Season* (Grand Rapids: Eerdmans & Edinburgh: St. Andrew's Press, 1994) p.42; *The Gospel in a Pluralist Society* (London: SPCK, 1989) p.222.

11. P. Meadows and J. Steinberg, *That's Y Jesus Came* (Milton Keynes: Word, 2001).

Chapter Two

1. C. Turnbull, *The Forest People* (London: Cape, 1961) pp.227–8.
2. Quoted in J.R.W. Stott, *The Message of 2 Timothy* (Leicester & Downers Grove: Inter-Varsity Press, 1973) p.77.
3. Greek word *orthotomeō*, J.R.W. Stott, *ibid.*, pp.67–68.
4. J. Wesley, 'The Repentance of Believers', in *Sermons on Several Occasions* (London: Wesleyan Methodist Book Room, undated) p.175.
5. J.I. Packer, *A Passion for Holiness* (Leicester: Crossway, 1992) p.212.
6. *Ibid.*, p.33.
7. T.C. Oden, *First and Second Timothy and Titus* (Louisville: John Knox Press, 1989) p.72.
8. See D. Guthrie, *The Pastoral Epistles* (Leicester: Inter-Varsity Press, 1977) p.141, and T.C. Oden *ibid.*, pp.164–5. Both commentators speak of the rule of the Olympics that all competitors were required to complete ten months of strict training before they were permitted to participate in the games.
9. A. Wallis, *Into Battle* (Alresford: Christian Literature Crusade and Eastbourne: Kingsway, 1983) p.74.
10. *Reader's Digest* (November 2004) p.115.
11. The meaning of the verb *kopiaō*. (D. Guthrie, *ibid.*, p.141).
12. The Chalcedonian Definition, AD 451, from H. Bettenson, *Documents of the Christian Church* (Oxford: Oxford University Press, 2nd edn. 1963) p.51.

Chapter Three

1. W. Hendriksen, *1 & 2 Timothy and Titus* (London: The Banner of Truth Trust, 1960) p.282.
2. E.F. Scott, *The Pastoral Epistles* (London: Hodder & Stoughton, 1936) p.119.

3. J. Calvin, *Commentaries* , Vol. 21, quoted in T.C. Oden, *First and Second Timothy and Titus* (Louisville: John Knox Press, 1989) p.75. Emphasis original.

4. D. Bonhoeffer, *The Cost of Discipleship* (London: SCM, 1959) p.78.

5. Quoted in G. Leibholz, 'Memoir', in *The Cost of Discipleship*, p.16.

6. L. Newbigin, 'Context and Conversion', in *International Review of Mission* 68 no. 271, July 1979, p.308.

7. © 1993 Make Way Music, verse 3. Used with permission.

8. Reported in the *Christian Herald* , 28 February 2004, p.3.

9. J. Eldredge, *Wild at Heart: Discovering the Secret of a Man's Soul* (Nashville: Thomas Nelson, 2001) p.149.

10. D. Bonhoeffer, *The Cost of Discipleship, ibid.*, p.82.

Chapter Four

1. T.C. Oden, *First and Second Timothy and Titus* (Louisville: John Knox Press, 1989) p.136.

2. M. Muggeridge, *Jesus Rediscovered* (New York: Doubleday, 1979) Chapter 1. For the whole text, see http://www.worldinvisible.com /library/mugridge/jred/jredcont.htm.

3. C. Wesley, verse 2 of 'And Let This Feeble Body Frail', written in 1759, 1878 *Methodist Hymnal* no. 948.

4. Evangelical Alliance Commission on Unity and Truth Among Evangelicals (ACUTE), *The Nature of Hell* (Carlisle: Paternoster, 2000) p.117.

5. L. Newbigin, *The Other Side of 1984* (Geneva: World Council of Churches, 1983) p.1.

6. D. Bosch, *A Spirituality of the Road* (Scottdale: Herald Press, 1979) p.85.

National Distributors

UK: (and countries not listed below)
CWR, Waverley Abbey House, Waverley Lane, Farnham, Surrey GU9 8EP.
Tel: (01252) 784700 Outside UK +44 1252 784700

AUSTRALIA: CMC Australasia, PO Box 519, Belmont, Victoria 3216.
Tel: (03) 5241 3288

CANADA: Cook Communications Ministries, PO Box 98, 55 Woodslee Avenue,
Paris, Ontario N3L 3E5 Tel: 1800 263 2664

GHANA: Challenge Enterprises of Ghana, PO Box 5723, Accra.
Tel: (021) 222437/223249 Fax: (021) 226227

HONG KONG: Cross Communications Ltd, 1/F, 562A Nathan Road, Kowloon.
Tel: 2780 1188 Fax: 2770 6229

INDIA: Crystal Communications, 10-3-18/4/1, East Marredpalli, Secunderabad – 500026,
Andhra Pradesh
Tel/Fax: (040) 27737145

KENYA: Keswick Books and Gifts Ltd, PO Box 10242, Nairobi.
Tel: (02) 331692/226047 Fax: (02) 728557

MALAYSIA: Salvation Book Centre (M) Sdn Bhd, 23 Jalan SS 2/64,
47300 Petaling Jaya, Selangor.
Tel: (03) 78766411/78766797 Fax: (03) 78757066/78756360

NEW ZEALAND: CMC Australasia, PO Box 36015, Lower Hutt.
Tel: 0800 449 408 Fax: 0800 449 049

NIGERIA: FBFM, Helen Baugh House, 96 St Finbarr's College Road, Akoka, Lagos.
Tel: (01) 7747429/4700218/825775/827264

PHILIPPINES: OMF Literature Inc, 776 Boni Avenue, Mandaluyong City.
Tel: (02) 531 2183 Fax: (02) 531 1960

SINGAPORE: Armour Publishing Pte Ltd, Block 203A Henderson Road,
11–06 Henderson Industrial Park, Singapore 159546.
Tel: 6 276 9976 Fax: 6 276 7564

SOUTH AFRICA: Struik Christian Books, 80 MacKenzie Street,
PO Box 1144, Cape Town 8000.
Tel: (021) 462 4360 Fax: (021) 461 3612

SRI LANKA: Christombu Books, 27 Hospital Street, Colombo 1.
Tel: (01) 433142/328909

TANZANIA: CLC Christian Book Centre, PO Box 1384, Mkwepu Street, Dar es Salaam.
Tel/Fax (022) 2119439

USA: Cook Communications Ministries, PO Box 98, 55 Woodslee Avenue, Paris,
Ontario, N3L 3E5 Canada
Tel: 1800 263 2664

ZIMBABWE: Word of Life Books (Pvt) Ltd, Christian Media Centre, 8 Aberdeen Road,
Avondale, PO Box A480 Avondale, Harare, Zimbabwe
Tel: (04) 333355 or 091301188
For email addresses, visit the CWR website: www.cwr.org.uk

CWR is a registered charity – Number 294387

CWR is a limited company registered in England – Registration Number 1990308

Day and Residential Courses
Counselling Training
Leadership Development
Biblical Study Courses
Regional Seminars
Ministry to Women
Daily Devotionals
Books and Videos
Conference Centre

Trusted all Over the World

CWR HAS GAINED A WORLDWIDE reputation as a centre of excellence for Bible-based training and resources. From our headquarters at Waverley Abbey House, Farnham, England, we have been serving God's people for 40 years with a vision to help apply God's Word to everyday life and relationships. The daily devotional *Every Day with Jesus* is read by nearly a million readers an issue in more than 150 countries, and our unique courses in biblical studies and pastoral care are respected all over the world. Waverley Abbey House provides a conference centre in a tranquil setting.

For free brochures on our seminars and courses, conference facilities, or a catalogue of CWR resources, please contact us at the following address.

CWR, Waverley Abbey House, Waverley Lane, Farnham, Surrey GU9 8EP, UK

Telephone: +44 (0)1252 784700
Email: mail@cwr.org.uk
Website: www.cwr.org.uk

CWR CRUSADE FOR WORLD REVIVAL
Applying God's Word to everyday life and relationships

HERE & NOW

One of the most inspiring books on the Beatitudes you
will ever read. Rob Frost's fresh approach to the opening to
Christ's Sermon on the Mount relates these timeless truths
to our experiences in the twenty-first century. *Here & Now*
will challenge you emotionally, delight you intellectually and
strengthen you spiritually. Written in association with the *Here
& Now* theatrical production, on tour throughout the UK.

ISBN: 1-85345-236-X
£3.99 (plus p&p)

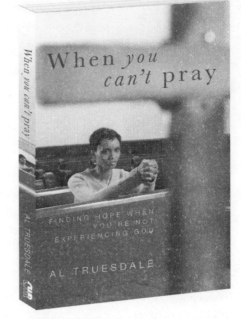

WHEN YOU CAN'T PRAY

'God …is not frightened by honest people, we will give voice to those who cannot pray.'
Al Truesdale

· Biblical teaching on a common problem
· Identifies barriers to prayer
· Enables and encourages new ways to pray

ISBN: 1-85345-349-8
£7.99 (plus p&p)

WHAT EVERY CHRISTIAN OUGHT TO KNOW

'I hope that the questions I am ascribing to my readers and attempting to answer at least "scratch" where my readers are "itching".' Richard S. Taylor

· Bible answers to questions of the Faith
· Bible based
· Straightforward question and answer approach
· Grow in your spiritual life
· Be transformed by the renewing of your mind

Richard S. Taylor was Professor of Theology at Nazerene Theological Seminary for 14 years and is an author of a range of books.

ISBN: 1-85345-316-1
£6.99 (plus p&p)

Prices correct at time of printing